ROSIE O'DONNELL

ROSIE O'DONNELL

Fran Donato

Therese De Angelis
Contributing Editor

CHELSEA HOUSE PUBLISHERS
PHILADELPHIA

Frontis: O'Donnell joins her look-alike audience shortly before the taping of The Rosie O'Donnell Show, *November 14, 1996. Audience members were selected from more than 2,000 people vying for a spot on that day's show.*

Chelsea House Publishers
EDITOR IN CHIEF Stephen Reginald
PRODUCTION MANAGER Pamela Loos
DIRECTOR OF PHOTOGRAPHY Judy L. Hasday
ART DIRECTOR Sara Davis
MANAGING EDITOR James D. Gallagher
SENIOR PRODUCTION EDITOR Lisa Chippendale

Staff for **Rosie O'Donnell**
SENIOR EDITOR Therese De Angelis
ASSOCIATE ART DIRECTOR/COVER DESIGN Takeshi Takahashi
DESIGNER Keith Trego
PICTURE RESEARCHER Sandy Jones
COVER ILLUSTRATION Bonnie T. Gardner

The Chelsea House World Wide Web site address is
www.chelseahouse.com

3 5 7 9 8 6 4 2

Library of Congress Cataloging-in-Publication Data

Donato, Fran.
Rosie O'Donnell / Fran Donato, Therese De Angelis.
128 pp. cm. — (Women of achievement)
Filmography: p. 121
Includes bibliographical references and index.
Summary: Presents the life and career of comic, actress, and talk-show
host Rosie O'Donnell.

ISBN 0-7910-4710-5. — ISBN 0-7910-4711-3 (pbk.)

1. O'Donnell, Rosie—Juvenile literature. 2. Comedians—United States—Biography—
Juvenile literature. 3. Motion picture actors and actresses—United States—Biography—
Juvenile literature. 4. Television personalities—United States—Biography—Juvenile
literature. [1. O'Donnell, Rosie. 2. Comedians. 3. Entertainers. 4. Women—Biography.]
I. De Angelis, Therese. II. Title. III. Series.
PN2287.O27D66 1998
792.7'028'092—dc21   98-25786
                                                                          CIP
                                                                          AC

CONTENTS

WOMEN of ACHIEVEMENT

Jane Addams
SOCIAL WORKER

Madeleine Albright
STATESWOMAN

Marian Anderson
SINGER

Susan B. Anthony
WOMAN SUFFRAGIST

Clara Barton
AMERICAN RED CROSS FOUNDER

Margaret Bourke-White
PHOTOGRAPHER

Rachel Carson
BIOLOGIST AND AUTHOR

Cher
SINGER AND ACTRESS

Hillary Rodham Clinton
FIRST LADY AND ATTORNEY

Katie Couric
JOURNALIST

Diana, Princess of Wales
HUMANITARIAN

Emily Dickinson
POET

Elizabeth Dole
POLITICIAN

Amelia Earhart
AVIATOR

Gloria Estefan
SINGER

Jodie Foster
ACTRESS AND DIRECTOR

Betty Friedan
FEMINIST

Althea Gibson
TENNIS CHAMPION

Ruth Bader Ginsburg
SUPREME COURT JUSTICE

Helen Hayes
ACTRESS

Katharine Hepburn
ACTRESS

Mahalia Jackson
GOSPEL SINGER

Helen Keller
HUMANITARIAN

**Ann Landers/
Abigail Van Buren**
COLUMNISTS

Barbara McClintock
BIOLOGIST

Margaret Mead
ANTHROPOLOGIST

Edna St. Vincent Millay
POET

Julia Morgan
ARCHITECT

Toni Morrison
AUTHOR

Grandma Moses
PAINTER

Lucretia Mott
WOMAN SUFFRAGIST

Sandra Day O'Connor
SUPREME COURT JUSTICE

Rosie O'Donnell
ENTERTAINER AND COMEDIAN

Georgia O'Keeffe
PAINTER

Eleanor Roosevelt
DIPLOMAT AND HUMANITARIAN

Wilma Rudolph
CHAMPION ATHLETE

Elizabeth Cady Stanton
WOMAN SUFFRAGIST

Harriet Beecher Stowe
AUTHOR AND ABOLITIONIST

Barbra Streisand
ENTERTAINER

Elizabeth Taylor
ACTRESS AND ACTIVIST

Mother Teresa
HUMANITARIAN AND
RELIGIOUS LEADER

Barbara Walters
JOURNALIST

Edith Wharton
AUTHOR

Phyllis Wheatley
POET

Oprah Winfrey
ENTERTAINER

Babe Didrikson Zaharias
CHAMPION ATHLETE

"REMEMBER THE LADIES"

MATINA S. HORNER

"Remember the Ladies." That is what Abigail Adams wrote to her husband John, then a delegate to the Continental Congress, as the Founding Fathers met in Philadelphia to form a new nation in March of 1776. "Be more generous and favorable to them than your ancestors. Do not put such limited power in the hands of the Husbands. If particular care and attention is not paid to the Ladies," Abigail Adams warned, "we are determined to foment a Rebellion, and will not hold ourselves bound by any Laws in which we have no voice, or Representation."

The words of Abigail Adams, one of the earliest American advocates of women's rights, were prophetic. Because when we have not "remembered the ladies," they have, by their words and deeds, reminded us so forcefully of the omission that we cannot fail to remember them. For the history of American women is as interesting and varied as the history of our nation as a whole. American women have played an integral part in founding, settling, and building our country. Some we remember as remarkable women who—against great odds—achieved distinction in the public arena: Anne Hutchinson, who in the 17th century became a charismatic religious leader; Phillis Wheatley, an 18th-century black slave who became a poet; Susan B. Anthony, whose name is synonymous with the 19th-century women's rights movement, and who led the struggle to enfranchise women; and in the 20th century, Amelia Earhart, the first woman to cross the Atlantic Ocean by air.

These extraordinary women certainly merit our admiration, but other women, "common women," many of them all but forgotten, should also be recognized for their contributions to American thought and culture. Women have been community builders; they have founded schools and formed voluntary associations to help those in need; they have assumed the major responsibility for rearing children, passing on from one generation to the next the values that keep a culture alive. These and innumerable other contributions, once ignored, are now being recognized by scholars, students, and the public. It is exciting and gratifying that a part of our history that was hardly acknowledged a few generations ago is now being studied and brought to light.

In recent decades, the field of women's history has grown from obscurity to a politically controversial splinter movement to academic respectability, in many cases mainstreamed into such traditional disciplines as history, economics, and psychology. Scholars of women, both female and male, have organized research centers at such prestigious institutions as Wellesley College, Stanford University, and the University of California. Other notable centers for women's studies are the Center for the American Woman and Politics at the Eagleton Institute of Politics at Rutgers University; the Henry A. Murray Research Center for the Study of Lives, at Radcliffe College; and the Women's Research and Education Institute, the research arm of the Congressional Caucus on Women's Issues. Other scholars and public figures have established archives and libraries, such as the Schlesinger Library on the History of Women in America, at Radcliffe College, and the Sophia Smith Collection, at Smith College, to collect and preserve the written and tangible legacies of women.

From the initial donation of the Women's Rights Collection in 1943, the Schlesinger Library grew to encompass vast collections documenting the manifold accomplishments of American women. Simultaneously, the women's movement in general and the academic discipline of women's studies in particular also began with a narrow definition and gradually expanded their mandate. Early causes, such as woman suffrage and social reform, abolition, and organized labor were joined by newer concerns, such as the history of women in business and the professions and in politics and government; the study of the family; and social issues such as health policy and education.

Women, as historian Arthur M. Schlesinger, jr., once pointed out, "have constituted the most spectacular casualty of traditional history. They have made up at least half the human race, but you could never tell that by looking at the books historians write." The new breed of historians is remedying that omission. They have written books about immigrant women and about working-class women who struggled for survival in cities and about black women who met the challenges of life in rural areas. They are telling the stories of women who, despite the barriers of tradition and economics, became lawyers and doctors and public figures.

The women's studies movement has also led scholars to question traditional interpretations of their respective disciplines. For example, the study of war has traditionally been an exercise in military and political analysis, an examination of strategies planned and executed by men. But scholars of women's history have pointed out that wars have also been periods of tremendous change and even opportunity for women, because the very absence of men on the home front enabled them to expand their educational, economic, and professional activities and to assume leadership in their homes.

The early scholars of women's history showed a unique brand of courage in choosing to investigate new subjects and take new approaches to old ones. Often, like their subjects, they endured criticism and even ostracism by their academic colleagues. But their efforts have unquestionably been worthwhile, because with the publication of each new study and book another piece of the historical patchwork is sewn into place, revealing an increasingly comprehensive picture of the role of women in our rich and varied history.

Such books on groups of women are essential, but books that focus on the lives of individuals are equally indispensable. Biographies can be inspirational, offering their readers the example of people with vision who have looked outside themselves for their goals and have often struggled against great obstacles to achieve them. Marian Anderson, for instance, had to overcome racial bigotry in order to perfect her art and perform as a concert singer. Isadora Duncan defied the rules of classical dance to find true artistic freedom. Jane Addams had to break down society's notions of the proper role for women in order to create new social situations, notably the settlement house. All of these women had to come to terms both with themselves and with the world in which they lived. Only then could they move ahead as pioneers in their chosen callings.

Biography can inspire not only by adulation but also by realism. It helps us to see not only the qualities in others that we hope to emulate, but also, perhaps, the weaknesses that made them "human." By helping us identify with the subject on a more personal level they help us feel that we, too, can achieve such goals. We read about Eleanor Roosevelt, for instance, who occupied a unique and seemingly enviable position as the wife of the president. Yet we can sympathize with her inner dilemma; an inherently shy woman, she had to force herself to live a most public life in order to use her position to benefit others. We may not be able to imagine ourselves having the immense poetic talent of Emily Dickinson, but from her story we can understand the challenges faced by a creative woman who was expected to fulfill many family responsibilities. And though few of us will ever reach the level of athletic accomplishment displayed by Wilma Rudolph or Babe Zaharias, we can still appreciate their spirit, their overwhelming will to excel.

A biography is a multifaceted lens. It is first of all a magnification, the intimate examination of one particular life. But at the same time, it is a wide-angle lens, informing us about the world in which the subject lived. We come away from reading about one life knowing more about the social, political, and economic fabric of the time. It is for this reason, perhaps, that the great New England essayist Ralph Waldo Emerson wrote in 1841, "There is properly no history: only biography." And it is also why biography, and particularly women's biography, will continue to fascinate writers and readers alike.

Accompanied by an actor from the cast of Broadway's Beauty and the Beast, *Tony Awards host Rosie O'Donnell performs an opening number at the 51st annual awards in June 1997.*

EVERYBODY LOVES ROSIE

Maybe you've seen her on network or cable television, like VH-1, Nickelodeon, or HBO. Perhaps you've seen her in such movies as *A League of Their Own* or *Harriet the Spy.* You may even have watched her perform onstage, in the Broadway musical *Grease!* or in one of her original comedy routines. Or maybe you've only read about her in newspapers, magazines, or books. In any case, if you like entertainment, chances are you know about Rosie O'Donnell.

The actress, comedian, single mother, and producer of her own nationally syndicated daytime talk show has kept herself in the entertainment spotlight since she was a teenager. The woman who has been labeled "the Queen of Nice" has soared to the top of the list of current daytime talk-show hosts, second only to Oprah Winfrey, and she won an Emmy Award for Best Talk Show Host in 1997 and two Emmy nominations in 1998. Mimi Udovitch of *Us* magazine attributes O'Donnell's success to her "knack . . . for being both star and regular gal," a quality that makes it easy for audience members and TV viewers to imagine themselves in her place. A star in her own right, Rosie O'Donnell remains at heart a starstruck fan.

Rosie first thought about hosting her own talk show in 1993, when late-night host David Letterman left NBC for CBS. She was among those whom NBC considered as a replacement for Letterman (the network eventually hired Conan O'Brien). The following year, CBS also considered Rosie as a regular substitute host for Letterman himself. In 1995, she filled in briefly for Kathie Lee Gifford on the morning program *Live with Regis and Kathie Lee*, and she enjoyed the experience so much that she began seriously considering having her own show. According to James Robert Parish in *Rosie: Rosie O'Donnell's Biography* (1997), she told her agent, Risa Shapiro, that doing a show similar to the morning show would be fun. "[I]t's interesting, you get to talk to celebrities. It's not depressing, like Ricki Lake and the guy who slept with the mother's father or whatever." Shapiro agreed to make inquiries, and in November 1995, Rosie signed a contract with Warner Bros. television, making her the star and executive producer of a new talk show that would run for at least 39 weeks and would pay Rosie an estimated $4 million over four years. At 10:00 A.M. on Monday, June 10, 1996, the 34-year-old comedian began broadcasting the first *Rosie O'Donnell Show*.

Rosie immediately began promoting her show to local TV stations across America, promising executives that "there will be no fist fights" on her program. O'Donnell managed to make deals with 166 stations covering 93 percent of the United States.

Rosie's goal was to recreate the kind of TV talk show that she loved to watch while she was growing up. She wanted to follow in the footsteps of popular talk-show hosts such as Steve Allen, Johnny Carson, Merv Griffin, Dinah Shore, and Mike Douglas. She was not interested in focusing on sensational topics or in discussing personal problems with angry or humiliated guests. Calling herself "Merv Griffin for the '90s," Rosie explained her aim for *The Rosie O'Donnell Show*:

Merv Griffin, host of The Merv Griffin Show, *which ran almost continuously from 1962 to 1986. Watching the show with her mother and grandmother was an afternoon ritual for young Rosie, and Griffin was her prime model for* The Rosie O'Donnell Show, *which premiered in June 1996.*

I'm trying to bring back the kind of show that I grew up watching—the kind of show that brought the entertainers that I loved into my living room every day. The kind of show that I could watch with my grandmother and my little sister, and everyone got something out of it. And that's what I'm trying to do. I don't think I'm trying to save TV, or be the antithesis of sleaze TV shows. . . . I do genuinely have an appreciation of celebrities, of talent, of musicals.

Most appealing to O'Donnell about the programs she watched as a child was that no guest ever seemed uncomfortable. Of Merv Griffin's show, she said, "It appeared everyone was his friend and nobody felt [like they were] in dangerous territory." She believed that American television audiences would enjoy that type of programming again.

Rosie's choice of guests clearly illustrates this conviction: David Cassidy and Susan Dey of the 1970s TV show *The Partridge Family;* Donny Osmond of the 1970s brother-and-sister variety show *Donny and Marie;* soap-opera star Susan Lucci of *All My Children;* Marlo Thomas of *That Girl;* Maureen McCormick of *The Brady Bunch;* Cheryl Ladd and Kate Jackson of *Charlie's Angels;* film star Sylvester Stallone of *Rocky* fame; Henry Winkler, "the Fonz" on TV's *Happy Days;* and Michael J. Fox of the 1980s sitcom *Family Ties.* The process of selecting guests is far from scientific. "When I say that I want to have somebody on the show, and the producer asks, 'Why?' I'll tell you why. It's because they did this series and that series and I remember this Movie of the Week, and I think they're great," says O'Donnell.

From her first show it was clear that Rosie O'Donnell would set herself apart from other talk-show hosts. Not only is she the host but she is also an admirer of each of her guests. "I have always felt more like an audience member than a performer," she once said. John McDaniel, the musical director of *The Rosie O'Donnell Show* and also Rosie's friend, describes her reactions to her guests as completely genuine. "She's totally real," he says of her enthusiasm. "It's heightened for TV, but not much. . . . She's really goo-goo ga-ga about these people. It's hilarious."

And because Rosie is a fan of those who appear on her show, she knows who her guests are and why they are on her show that day. Unlike some hosts who have little time to study the information from pre-show interviews, Rosie has usually seen every movie or TV show her guests have done. In fact, she often knows the words to the theme songs from those shows as well.

Probably the most important reasons for Rosie's switch from movie actress and stand-up comedian to daytime talk-show host are her adopted children, Parker Jaren (born in 1995) and Chelsea Belle (born in 1997). The show's regular taping schedule gives her more time to spend with them each day. It was certainly more appealing than the prospect of taking them on the road to continue her career as a comedian and actress, where they would spend most of their time in a nursery without seeing her. By the time *The Rosie O'Donnell Show* debuted, Rosie had a ready answer for those who questioned why she put aside her other aspirations to have more time with Parker. "The reason is indefinable but quite easy to feel. I don't worry about answering [those questions] so much now. I just ask a question myself. I say, 'Do you have kids?' When [people] say no, I say, 'That's why you're asking.'"

Motherhood has indeed altered O'Donnell's show-business schedule. Before she adopted Parker in May 1995, her life was filled with appearances at stand-up comedy clubs and charity events, and on-location movie shoots required that she travel across the country and work odd hours for a good part of each year. Raising children while keeping such a demanding and irregular schedule seemed irresponsible to O'Donnell. In her television studio offices, her kids have their own nursery, so mother and children are always near one another.

O'Donnell has always had great love and compassion for children, and as a celebrity, she feels compelled to use her fame to help them in any way she can. "When I was a kid I was influenced so much by movie stars and TV moms," she told *Good Housekeeping* magazine in June 1997. "I found a lot of solace and guidance from them. So the fact that I can now have a positive effect on kids is wonderful." O'Donnell has established her own charity organization, the For All Kids Foundation, to fund day care centers across the country, and she keeps herself and her huge TV audience up to date on the latest national fund-raising organizations for children.

"[W]hen you have celebrity in America," Rosie explained in a December 1997 interview with *Radiance* magazine, "you also have a tremendous amount of power and influence, and you have to make a conscious decision about how you're going to use that power." One of the ways she plans to do so is by helping to institute a "national day care system" in America that would set universal standards and registration requirements even for day care centers run from private homes. She feels that such regulations are "appropriate for the people who are taking care of [the] next generation of citizens."

But her commitment doesn't end there—*The Rosie O'Donnell Show* has earned a reputation for giving a nationwide voice to many local and regional charities and organizations in America, which range in purpose from feeding the hungry and curing diseases to providing shelter for animals. She fully understands the power of fame and knows that being able to reach millions of people every day is a serious responsibility.

Rosie O'Donnell believes that the origin of her strong humanitarian feelings is in her childhood experiences. "I grew up in a home that was not ideal," she has said. "We were neglected in many ways. I always knew that I had an affinity for children, and I had a desire to touch and inspire them in the way that entertainers touched and inspired and provided me solace in a less than happy childhood."

O'Donnell's reputation as the Queen of Nice is the result of years of hard work and perseverance. Her seemingly idyllic early childhood was shattered by the illness and death of her mother in 1973. Forced by circumstance to become the family caretaker at age 11, O'Donnell knows too well the importance of providing love, support, and comfort to other youngsters. "So if there's anything I want to do with my celebrity," she says, "it's to make the world a safer place for kids."

Both Rosie O'Donnell and her mother, Roseann, were ardent fans of singer and actress Barbra Streisand, shown here in the 1968 movie Funny Girl.

2

FUNNY GIRL

The entertainer we know as "Rosie" was born Roscann O'Donnell on March 21, 1962, the third child of Edward and Roseann O'Donnell. The O'Donnells ultimately had five children: Eddie, Danny, Roseann, and Maureen, each born one year apart, and Timmy, who is three years younger than Maureen. Edward O'Donnell was among the many Irish immigrants who settled on Long Island, New York, in the early decades of the 20th century. He came with his parents from Donegal, Ireland, when he was a child. In his mid-twenties, Edward married a beautiful blue-eyed, black-haired woman named Roseann Murtha, the only child of Daniel and Kathryn Murtha. The Murthas were also Irish, but Roseann had been born in America.

Edward and Roseann O'Donnell and their children lived in a two-story brick house on Rhonda Lane in a town called Commack, "exit 52 off the Long Island Expressway," as area locals know it. In a 1993 interview by her good friend Madonna for *Mademoiselle* magazine, Rosie jokingly described her middle-class hometown: "Tract row houses one after another, exactly the same. Different-colored shutters were the only way you could tell them apart." One of Rosie's former classmates fondly remembers their hometown in a 1997 biography of Rosie O'Donnell by George Mair and Anna Green. The former Commack resident recalled, "We all used to leave our doors unlocked, and we walked to the buses by ourselves. It was the kind of town . . . where the grandparents lived with their families." Like a lot of kids growing up in suburbia during that time, Rosie spent her early childhood in a safe, nurturing environment.

Rhonda Lane was a pleasant, tree-lined street with front lawns and side yards where the neighborhood kids could play. Nearby was Commack's public park, Hoyt Farm, covering about 100 acres of land. At one time it even housed farm animals as well as playground equipment. When the O'Donnell kids were growing up, the town was populated mostly by large Irish-American and Italian-American families, so they had plenty of companions. Rosie herself was very active in neighborhood games. "I played softball, volleyball, kickball, tennis, and basketball; a regular tomboy jock girl and proud of it. . . . I was always the first girl picked for the neighborhood teams," she remembers proudly. "I got picked ahead of my three brothers, which I think still affects them. I always had time for a good game." She describes herself more bluntly in her stand-up comedy routine: "I was a tomboy—is that a shock to anyone? I didn't do ballet."

Edward O'Donnell was an electrical engineer who worked for the Grumman Corporation, where he helped design cameras for surveillance satellites that were contracted by the U.S. government. During the 1960s, the Cold War between the United States and the U.S.S.R. was in full bloom, and Rosie remembers her father telling her that the advanced technology of the Soviets allowed them to read the license plates of cars in America, using spy cameras like the ones he designed. In her comedy act, Rosie laughingly replied, "'Thanks, Dad. That's a comforting thought for an eight-year-old.' I'm in the bathroom thinking, 'They can probably see this in Russia.'" She also joked that her father was "very depressed" when the Berlin Wall, which divided democratic West Germany and Communist East Germany, was destroyed in 1989, because it signaled the end of such intense international surveillance.

Roseann O'Donnell was president of the local Parent-Teacher Association (PTA), and she connected with young Rosie in a special way. "My mother was very funny—she did the equivalent of stand-up at PTA meetings—she made all the teachers laugh," Rosie remembers. "When she came to visit the school and walked down the halls, all the teachers would come out of their classrooms to talk to her. So I knew she had this thing people wanted—that people would go to her, because of this comedy thing." Rosie inherited her mother's lively sense of humor and used it herself in social situations.

Roseann also shared many of her interests with her daughter. Rosie credits her mother with having cultivated her own love of musical theater. The two often spent time together listening to soundtracks from Broadway shows. "I'd listen to *Oklahoma!* over and over, and I'd wait every year for *The Sound of Music* and *Mary Poppins* to come on television," Rosie has said. She became so enchanted by the music and characters from these Broadway productions that she would sometimes sing show tunes during show-and-tell periods in school. "Other kids are bringing in Barbie dolls," Rosie joked, "and I'm singing *Oklahoma!*"

The O'Donnells had little money to spare while their children were young. "We didn't have many luxuries," Rosie claims. "We didn't have matching socks. Or top sheets for the bed, just the bottom sheet. We didn't have a blow dryer, we used an Electrolux vacuum cleaner with the hose on the turn-around side." The money the O'Donnells did save was spent carefully. Vacations, for example, were less than luxurious. "My mom and dad would pile all of us kids in the station wagon and drive up to Niagara Falls. . . . Twelve hours of driving with five little kids and two irate parents," she dryly remarks. Her parents' frugality made an impression on Rosie, who declares that she is still thrifty despite her wealth and success.

Among Rosie's favorite childhood rituals was sitting down with her mother and maternal grandmother, Kathryn Murtha (who lived with the O'Donnells), to watch weekday afternoon talk and variety shows hosted by Merv Griffin and Mike Douglas. Because the television was almost always on in the O'Donnell home, much of the family's time together was spent watching favorite TV shows. "My whole family knew the entire fall schedule before it even went on the air," Rosie claims. "We had the *Newsday* supplement and we'd memorize what was on. We were a huge, huge, huge TV family."

But afternoon TV wasn't enough for Rosie. She went to great lengths to watch late-night programs like *The Tonight Show*. Many times, after her parents had sent the children to bed, Rosie would "sneak down and watch Johnny Carson from the stairs." After the program ended she would sneak back upstairs, where she often hid out in the bathroom and pretended to be Carson's guest while speaking to the bathroom mirror. "I would say, as if I [were] thirty, 'You know, Johnny, when I was twelve, I used to sit in my bathroom and talk to you.'"

Another favorite was *The Carol Burnett Show*, a popular weekly variety hour featuring a regular cast of multitalented performers including Harvey Korman, Lyle Waggoner, Vicki Lawrence, and, in later years, Tim Conway. Each week, Burnett and cast members sang, danced, and acted in hilarious skits that often left the audience—and the rest of the cast—reeling with laughter. The program inspired the tomboyish Rosie because Carol Burnett's humor, talent, and offbeat beauty

Young Rosie was drawn to TV sitcoms featuring independent female leads. Among her favorite TV characters was Mary Richards, played by Mary Tyler Moore (with cast member Ted Knight on the left) in The Mary Tyler Moore Show.

proved that a woman didn't have to look like a Barbie doll to be successful and well liked.

Rosie also faithfully watched other popular shows with female leads, like *I Dream of Jeannie* and *Bewitched*. She was especially impressed with two actresses: Marlo Thomas, who played the title character in *That Girl*, one of the first TV sitcoms to feature a single working woman; and Mary Tyler Moore, who starred in one of Rosie's all-time favorite TV programs, *The Mary Tyler Moore Show*. Rosie was such an ardent fan of the latter that for years she kept a notebook filled with the minute details of each episode. When the adult Rosie featured Mary Tyler Moore as a guest on her talk show, Rosie knew more about each episode than Moore herself could remember.

There seemed to be no limit to Rosie's passion for TV trivia. "I annoyed my family my whole life," she has declared. "They were always trying to get me to shut up." She remembers telling her family that she was going to be a movie star. "So they always knew what I wanted to do," she says. "I just don't think they ever thought I would do it."

Now the host of her own talk show, Rosie has fulfilled at least one dream: she has honored nearly all of her childhood TV idols, from Merv Griffin to Mary Tyler Moore, either by speaking about them on the air or by having them as guests. While growing up, Rosie collected scores of toys associated with popular TV shows—but unlike many other fans, she still has most of them and proudly displays them on her show to guests who have had their likenesses made into dolls or featured on the side of a kids' lunch box.

Rosie's interest in the performing arts was not limited to television, however. The O'Donnells tried to expose their children to as much live entertainment as their budget would allow. For example, Rosie was six years old when she saw her first musical—a production of *George M* (about actor, songwriter, and producer George M. Cohan) at the Westbury Music Fair on Long Island.

There she also attended her first pop concert, starring the brother-and-sister team the Carpenters. She was impressed by singer Karen Carpenter, who not only sang but also had started out as the drummer for the band. O'Donnell vividly remembers not only the concert but also the long wait outside the Westbury Music Fair, where she hoped to catch a glimpse of the singer. When Karen Carpenter passed by, Rosie "reached through the fence and touched her sweater. It was . . . a big thing for me," she recalls. In an effort to emulate Carpenter, Rosie learned to play the drums, practicing in the family garage. She still plays quite well.

On special occasions, Mrs. O'Donnell took her

daughter to New York City to watch movies at the famous Radio City Music Hall, where some of the world's most renowned entertainers have performed regularly. Before each showing, Rosie was dazzled by an elaborate stage production featuring a group of high-kicking female dancers known as the Rockettes. Sitting in the Radio City balcony sharing a box of lemon-drop candy with her mother remains one of Rosie O'Donnell's most cherished memories.

Barbra Streisand was by far Rosie's and her mother's favorite Broadway performer. Mrs. O'Donnell was such a fan that she would plan her family's schedule around events like a Streisand TV special or the release of a new

One of Rosie's childhood idols: comedian and actor Carol Burnett (center), with cast members Harvey Korman (left) and Vicki Lawrence on The Carol Burnett Show.

movie. To this day, Rosie herself views the year 1968 as a turning point in her life: that's when the movie *Funny Girl*, starring Barbra Streisand, was released. Only six years old at the time, O'Donnell nevertheless claims that she already knew that what Streisand was doing on the big screen was exactly what she herself wanted to do.

A natural mimic, Rosie memorized the songs from her mother's collection of Streisand albums and movie soundtracks and performed them while imitating the singer. "I'd go into the kitchen singing 'Second Hand Rose' with Barbra's accent, and my mother would laugh and laugh. It was a great way to get attention, so I kept it up," she recalls. Her sister, Maureen, agrees. "Rosie was always telling jokes and doing imitations," she has said.

O'Donnell's first foray onto the stage came when she was in third grade. The class performed *The Wizard of Oz*, with Rosie as Glinda, the good witch. Rosie and Maureen had already spent many hours at home acting out the story, but because Maureen always played the part of Dorothy, Rosie wanted a chance to play the character in the school performance. Her teachers, on the other hand, thought that her talents would be better put to use in a more flamboyant role. "Jan Brenner got to be Dorothy, and I never got over it," O'Donnell recalls wryly. "I remember it like it was yesterday."

The grade-schooler did not limit her performing skills to the stage, however. Each show-and-tell period presented Rosie with a fresh opportunity to polish her "act." Unlike most of her peers, though, Rosie was interested in making adults—not fellow students— laugh. She had seen her mother work magic with PTA members and teachers, and she decided to pattern herself that way. "I was the teacher's pet because I could make teachers laugh," she says.

At home the situation was much the same. As the middle child of five, Rosie learned to use humor to get attention from adults. Family friends quickly detected her flair for entertaining and her talent for pulling off pranks that might land other kids in trouble. "I knew when I was four years old [that] I wanted to be in show business," Rosie has said. "There was no choice for me." And thanks to a passion for theater, movies, and popular TV shows instilled in Rosie by her earliest and most beloved fan, Roseann O'Donnell, she seemed headed for just that kind of career.

Rosie and her sister, Maureen, attending the premiere of A League of Their Own *in June 1992. After the death of their mother, Rosie became the maternal caretaker for the O'Donnell family. "Rosie has always protected me," Maureen has said of her older sister. "She is the one I always call when I have a tough day."*

3

CHANGED FOREVER

In December 1972, Roseann O'Donnell was diagnosed with terminal pancreatic and liver cancer. She was 37 years old. Before the O'Donnells, including Roseann herself, could adjust to hearing this dreadful news, Roseann's health rapidly began to deteriorate. She spent the next few months shuttling to and from Huntington Hospital, 20 miles from Commack, where she was repeatedly treated.

Rosie still remembers trying to visit her mother in the hospital. Even though children under 12 years old were not permitted to visit patients, a few sympathetic nurses allowed Rosie and her siblings to see their mother by sneaking them upstairs in a back elevator.

What made this ordeal even more bewildering for Roseann's children was the fact that Edward O'Donnell never told them what was ailing their mother. Steeped in denial over his wife's fate, he buried himself in work and began drinking heavily. He could not even bring himself to accept that Roseann was dying, let alone tell his children the news. Although they knew that their mother's condition was serious, none of them were consciously aware that she would never recover.

O'Donnell has said that she only learned what her mother died of years later, when she was 16. At first, she says, they were told that she had hepatitis, a disease marked by inflammation of the liver. She recalls:

> They thought that was a big word and kids wouldn't know. But I went to the library and looked it up, and it said it was a disease that you got from dirty needles [hepatitis can be spread through infected blood; for example, by sharing needles used to inject drugs]. I thought to myself it was from sewing. That's the kind of household it was—you had to draw your own conclusions, because you weren't really allowed to ask.

During the months when Roseann O'Donnell was in the hospital or bedridden at home, 10-year-old Rosie tried to maintain a sense of normalcy by taking on many of her mother's household chores. She also worked hard to distract her mother from her pain by continuing to entertain her with jokes and imitations. O'Donnell now admits that she also used humor as a shield against her own fear of losing her mother. "I refused to believe my mom was dying, and I wanted to keep her laughing," she recalls today.

On March 17, 1973, only four months after her condition was diagnosed and just four days before Rosie's 11th birthday, Roseann O'Donnell died. Edward, who had grown increasingly silent and withdrawn, was completely numb. He came home from the hospital and uttered only a few words to his perplexed children: "Your mother passed away."

"I didn't know what that meant," Rosie says. "And that was the end of the discussion." Edward dealt with his wife's death by avoiding the subject with his children. They knew nothing of the burial arrangements for their mother, and they were not even permitted to attend her funeral.

Shortly after Roseann's death, Edward O'Donnell took the children to Ireland for several weeks to introduce them to his relatives and friends. He believed that a change of scenery might be good for all of them. But what might have been a delightful vacation abroad under other circumstances was an unenjoyable break for the children, who were still grieving for their mother. Rosie herself recalls only fragments of the trip. "I remember eating salt and vinegar potato chips and having sweets," Rosie recalls. "We used to go to the woods and my cousin would shoot cap guns and we'd hide in the bushes and watch the helicopters come because we were in Belfast for part of it." She also remembers being teased by her siblings for having picked up "the brogue" (Irish accent) while there—and she developed a fascination with bagpipes, which she later learned to play.

After the O'Donnells returned home, Edward continued to cope with the loss of his wife in solitude. He discouraged his children from talking about her, and not long after Roseann's death he began to remove everything that had belonged to her from their home. When he sold her blue station wagon without warning, Rosie was heartbroken. She had taken to climbing into the car to be alone and think about her mother. "It still smelled like my mom," she remembers.

By the time Edward was through with this process, almost nothing remained of Roseann O'Donnell by which her children could remember her. "I only have two pictures of her and none of her things," Rosie says today. (She did manage to hold onto one of Roseann's rings, but it was stolen during a skiing trip in 1990.) Kept from talking about her mother and denied keepsakes, Rosie easily recalls the anguish surrounding her mother's death but does not have many clear memories of the woman herself.

Like many people who lose loved ones, Rosie sometimes had difficulty believing that her mother was irretrievably gone. At times, she would imagine that her mother was still alive, cheering her on from the stands during a basketball game, for example. She even entertained the fantasy that her mom had run off to California, or that she had been kidnapped—anything to avoid the finality of death.

But Rosie and her siblings also managed to find healthier ways to deal with their grief. They discovered that adopting their mother's sense of humor helped them to recover. "In my family being funny was a way you could communicate the truth without getting in trouble," Rosie says. "You couldn't say, 'I'm in a lot of pain and we don't talk about mom's death and we don't have the right clothes,' but you could make a joke. Like: 'Oh, this is a classy dinner. What are we having, Ode to Pea Pods again?'"

The O'Donnell kids also turned to one another for support. Having emotionally "lost" their father as well as their mother, they formed what Rosie has called "one functioning parent-children unit." Roseann O'Donnell had taught each of her children to cook a different meal after she learned that she was dying, and they now took turns preparing dinner every night. Each child also had specific household chores to do, usually assigned by Rosie. Even her older brothers, Eddie and Danny, took orders from their sister without complaint. "There were no specific role models assigned to the genders," Rosie says. "The boys had to cook and clean [too], and if there was a flat on the bike, somebody just had to fix it."

Still, with practically no parental restrictions, Rosie remembers, she and her siblings were "pretty wild, with little respect for authority." To her, being rebellious meant "that I was always the boss. . . . I always felt that I knew more than [adults]. I got away with that attitude because I was funny. I was lucky I wasn't prone to getting into trouble." Fortunately, friends and neighbors stepped in to help out. Rosie was often invited to stay at the home of her best friend, Jackie Ellard, who lived next door. The Ellards, Rosie says, "provided me with safety and the feeling of being nurtured,"

which she no longer felt in her own home. (Rosie still sends Bernice Ellard, Jackie's mother, an annual Christmas card, and Jackie herself now works for Rosie, sorting her fan mail.)

The O'Donnell children also received a great deal of support from teachers at school. Rosie says that they profoundly influenced her life during the years following her mother's death. Her eighth-grade math teacher, Pat Maravel, was especially helpful. Maravel "became a surrogate mom to me, she helped me stay

With her mother gone, Rosie took comfort in TV programs and movies that featured happy families, like the 1964 Walt Disney movie Mary Poppins. "They had the families I wished I had," she remembers.

focused and feel loved," Rosie says. "She took me under her wing and helped me through all those adolescent girl things." Her teachers' influence was so strong that O'Donnell claims she would have become a teacher herself had she not entered the entertainment field.

Another way Rosie coped with a motherless adolescence was by reading about other survivors of loss and misfortune. "I used to read books about tragic situations, people who had overcome insurmountable odds," she once said. "I read a lot of things about the Holocaust and mass murderers and people who had tragic accidents—just so I could face my fear."

Eddie, Danny, Rosie, Maureen, and Timmy also derived comfort from continuing some of the rituals they had established with their mother, like watching afternoon talk shows. "No other family in my neighborhood was as obsessed with TV as mine was," Rosie admitted. "We were allowed to watch TV twenty-four hours a day. And we did."

Watching the adventures of make-believe families on TV programs like *Nanny and the Professor*, *Eight Is Enough*, and *The Courtship of Eddie's Father* also eased Rosie's loneliness. "I liked all the shows with single parents," she says. "They represented what I was living." Other shows, like *The Waltons* and *The Brady Bunch*, featured intact families and fed Rosie's hope that her own family's heartaches would eventually end. Even the movies Rosie had come to know and love, such as *The Sound of Music*, *Mary Poppins*, and *Chitty Chitty Bang Bang*, now held more meaning. "[T]hey had the families I wished I had," she recalls— and their problems were always solved by the end of the show.

In addition to watching TV, Rosie made an extra effort to continue the tradition of going to the theater. Using her allowance and the money she saved from baby-sitting jobs, she saw Saturday afternoon

Rosie was so enamored of singer and actress Bette Midler that she skipped school one day in 1975 to see a Broadway performance of Midler's Clams on the Half Shell. *"She's really the reason I'm in entertainment,"* Rosie would say years later, introducing Midler to the studio audience of The Rosie O'Donnell Show.*

movies at the Westbury Music Fair and bought tickets to Broadway musicals such as *Pippin, Ain't Misbehavin', The Wiz,* and her all-time favorite, *Dreamgirls.* If she couldn't persuade a friend or relative to drive her, she would take a train to get there. At times, she would even cut classes to catch a Broadway matinee during the week.

Of all the performers Rosie saw onstage, Bette Midler made a particularly powerful impression. Rosie was so captivated by Midler's performance in the off-beat musical showcase *Clams on the Half Shell* (1975) that she immediately "wanted to be her. I didn't just want to be like her. I wanted to become her." The teenager was inspired by Midler's unconventional looks and her unique approach to making a name for herself in show business.

Bette Midler's performance may have captivated Rosie's spirit, but her enthusiasm for Barbra Streisand remained constant. Midler and Streisand both seemed undaunted by the odds against them; both were extremely talented women who overcame great difficulties to make it to the top of their field. But Streisand was Rosie's idol, and a direct link to her mother. At times, she even imagined that the performer and her widowed father would meet and marry.

The pain and confusion Rosie experienced over the loss of her mother forced her to think about what she wanted to do with her own life. Like many people who lose a parent when they are still young, Rosie struggled with the fear that she would not live past the age at which her mother died and, like her, would not have enough time to enjoy life fully. For this reason, she became determined to succeed before reaching her thirties, just in case she suffered a fate similar to that of her mother's.

What Rosie admired most about Streisand and other celebrities was the enormous influence they have over their fans. "When my mother died of cancer, I remember thinking if Barbra Streisand had gone on the *Tonight Show* and asked everyone to donate ten dollars to find a cure for the disease, there would be one," Rosie said. "Everyone loved her so much, they'd get millions of dollars. I knew there was power involved in fame. And I knew I wanted it."

O'Donnell admits that "many, many years of therapy" helped her heal, finally, from the pain of her mother's death. In 1997 she described its effect on her: "My whole life revolved around my mother's death. It changed who I was as a person."

"I don't know who I would be if my mother had lived," Rosie says, "but I would trade it all in to see."

Aspiring actress Rosie O'Donnell early in her career.

4

SURVIVING

To some people, Rosie O'Donnell the teenager may have seemed overly cocky and brash. Others thought she simply had a healthy measure of what some call the "New York tough girl" attitude. Whatever one believes about her outgoing nature, O'Donnell can probably attribute her current success in part to her never-give-up personality.

Rosie wryly describes her teenaged self as "Miss High-School everything. I was the prom queen. I was homecoming queen. I was class president. I was class clown. And something else . . . oh, Most School-Spirited, which comes in handy in life. You never know when you might have to do a cheer." Beneath her know-it-all exterior Rosie was, like many adolescents, insecure, self-conscious about her looks, and sometimes lonely. But she grew skillful at hiding these emotions, using humor as she had always done—as a screen.

Rosie's way of rebelling against adults was a bit different from that of most teens. "I didn't smoke or drink or have sex," she says. "I just went to comedy clubs at 15 and told everyone I was going to be a comedienne." She and her girlfriends often used false IDs to get into some of the comedy clubs and restaurant bars around Commack.

The legendary Radio City Music Hall in New York City, where Rosie and her mother spent afternoons watching movies and lively performances by the Rockettes. Rosie's love of the theater was inspired by these trips; her career goal was to become a Broadway performer.

One of the places the girls frequented was a restaurant called the Ground Round in Mineola, Long Island. Tuesdays were "open-mike" nights in the bar, when customers were urged to participate in amateur entertainment contests for a $50 prize. On a dare one Tuesday, Rosie took the stage. She didn't have a prepared routine; instead, wearing funny-looking glasses, she simply shouted out one-liners and jokes that she'd told her friends and family over the years. "I was sixteen and I looked like I was twelve," she recalls, "with this cute little haircut and big sweatshirt and sweatpants. . . . [T]he audience—grown-ups like my parents' age—were like, 'Look at this little kid with chutzpah.'" For her efforts, Rosie took home that night's prize.

"Wow," she remembers thinking, "this is easy."

Encouraged by this early success, Rosie continued to experiment by participating in open-mike nights at other restaurants and clubs in the area. "I had no act at all," she admits, relying instead on her sharp wit and those silly glasses. But audiences seemed to enjoy her, and she began to think that she could make a living doing comedy while she groomed herself for her real career, stage acting.

Roseann O'Donnell's passion for show business had fueled her daughter's desire to become an actress. Rosie believed that acting onstage allowed you to be more accessible to your fans. In a 1995 interview, she told cable TV talk-show host Al Roker that attending Broadway shows with her mother enabled her to see "real live people" who acted for a living. "I'd see movies, but I never met [film stars]," she said. "I didn't know where they lived, who they were—but I'd come to see a Broadway show, I'd stand outside the stage door and I saw the people who had just done the show. So that was really my first love, was to be a Broadway star."

On another occasion, she explained that although other stand-up comedians may have aspired to be like Johnny Carson, who opened each *Tonight Show* with a monologue, Rosie wanted to be a comic actress like Carol Burnett or Lucille Ball. "I wanted the funny roles," she claims. "I wanted to be Laverne . . . on *Happy Days*. Those were my dreams as a kid." (Today, one of Rosie's close friends is Penny Marshall, who played Laverne on the TV sitcom *Happy Days*, and then on its spinoff, *Laverne and Shirley*.)

Despite her many activities, Rosie did well academically, maintaining a B average at Commack High School South. She was a member of the student council and was elected class president in her senior year, in addition to being named prom queen and homecoming queen. She played the drums in a school musical

The late Gilda Radner (left) as Roseanne Rosannadana, with Jane Curtin. Rosie O'Donnell's first shot at becoming a professional comic came after she did an imitation of Radner's Saturday Night Live *character for her high school Senior Follies.*

group. She also played a number of sports, including softball, volleyball, tennis, and basketball, and she coached her younger brother Timmy's softball team. And, not surprisingly, she was a member of the school drama club.

The drama club would ultimately give Rosie her first shot at becoming a professional comic. In her final semester at Commack South, her class put on a show called the Senior Follies, which O'Donnell describes as "sort of like *Saturday Night Live* skits about the teachers." Rosie's bit was an imitation of *SNL* comedian Gilda Radner's character Roseanne Rosannadana.

In the crowd that night was the older brother of one of Rosie's classmates, a comedian who also owned an area club. After the show, he asked her whether she'd like a paying job doing stand-up in his club. Determined to become an actress, Rosie refused. But the man persisted. "Why don't you try it?" he asked her. Rosie gave in.

Her first few attempts at stand-up didn't go over well with the club's audiences. But Rosie didn't give up. "I didn't have any material, let alone an act," she admits, "so I came off [stage] and blamed it on the audience." After her third unsuccessful try, she realized that she needed to come up with a real act.

The day before her next appearance at the club, O'Donnell saw a new young comedian on *The Merv Griffin Show* named Jerry Seinfeld. She thought his act was funny, and the television audience loved it, so Rosie made some mental notes of his performance. When she went onstage the following night, she finally had a routine. "You know, I was on my way over here tonight and the car broke down," she began. "I opened up the hood and [said to myself] what am I looking for? A big on-off switch?" For the next few minutes, she continued to rattle off well-polished jokes, faithfully reproducing the timing and hand gestures she had seen the night before. The audience loved her.

Rosie left the stage beaming with pride and excited about her newfound success. But her satisfaction was short-lived. As she came offstage, a crowd of angry comedians who were waiting to do their own acts confronted her, demanding to know where she had heard the jokes she had just used. "I told them I'd heard Jerry Seinfeld do them on *The Merv Griffin Show*," Rosie remembers. "When they told me I couldn't do that, that I had to do my own material, I was crushed, devastated. I mean, I didn't have any idea how to go home and make up my own jokes."

The 16-year-old was unaware that as a rule, comics do not "borrow" one another's material. "I thought once a guy told his jokes on TV you were allowed to use them. I thought a joke was a joke," she said. "It never occurred to me that I was stealing." On the way home, the angry teenager decided she'd had enough. After all, she reasoned, "When you're an actress, they don't ask you to write the movie. . . . I thought they were ridiculous."

Before long, however, Rosie realized that she had become addicted to the laughter and applause she received from audiences who enjoyed her act. She began working to create original material, just as the comics had advised her that night, turning to a subject that she knew best and that her local audiences could relate to—her own life in a TV-watching, Irish Catholic family. Soon she was appearing at other area comedy clubs, such as the Round Table and the White Horse Inn.

Looking back at this period of her life, Rosie noted that her youthful cockiness enabled her to walk onstage night after night and perform:

> When you're that age, you have such a huge ego that you think you are the best thing in the world. That narcissistic immaturity served me very well, because when [audiences] didn't laugh—and they shouldn't have laughed, because I wasn't funny—I thought to myself, 'Well, this audience stinks!' I had that huge, impenetrable self-confidence that only a child can have. When I was 28 and had been on the road for ten years, I couldn't believe I had walked on stage and performed with no material. In hindsight, it's frightening to me. At the time, it wasn't frightening. It was empowering.

Rosie was still keeping her busy school schedule, helping out at home, and baby-sitting for scores of neighborhood kids while she was performing in clubs. The pressure of constantly inventing new material eventually began to wear on her, so she began working as an emcee rather than a comic at a few of the more casual comedy houses popping up throughout Long Island. Not only did Rosie earn more money this way ($15 a night versus $10 for a stand-up gig) but she was also under less pressure to create an extended act of her own. She could be more herself, bantering with the audience and introducing other acts.

Emceeing provided an additional benefit: Rosie was able to "sit on the sidelines," watching and learning from other comedians. Many of the most popular ones took their own experiences and translated them into the universal language of humor. "They'd take an experience from their life that was relatable. They put the humor into it and presented it to the audience, who would go, 'Oh, yeah, I've done that.'"

Despite the advantages of an early introduction to show business, O'Donnell sometimes regrets having worked so hard during her teens. "Every single weekend of my life from the time I was 17 . . . I've been in a nightclub or a comedy club," she recalled years later. "It's never being out with friends on New Year's Eve—it's being in a club with 300 strangers. I was working nearly every holiday and every weekend [for years]."

In June 1980, Rosie graduated from Commack High School South. Although she was still determined to make it in show business—in her yearbook a fellow senior wrote, "say hello to Johnny Carson when you're a big star"—her father thought it was important that she have a college education before venturing into what seemed to be a precarious line of work.

Rosie's high-school grades may not have been the best, but she was a likeable, well-rounded student who had participated in a number of activities and had earned several popular honors, so she was an attractive candidate to a number of smaller colleges. Among the schools that offered her a financial scholarship was Dickinson College in Carlisle, Pennsylvania, about a four-hour drive from Commack. Rosie accepted. For the first time in years, she would be taking care of no one but herself.

As part of a work-study program, Rosie put in several hours each week in the college's administration office, where she quickly became a favorite of the full-time employees. A natural athlete, she fared well in physical education classes and sports like softball. Some weekends, she and a friend would catch a bus to Philadelphia, two hours away, where they would sight-see and visit the city's clubs. The trips were another means by which Rosie could stay in touch with the entertainment world.

When it came to fulfilling college course requirements, however, Rosie was unsuccessful. She felt out of place in Dickinson's academic environment, and her involvement in nonacademic pursuits left little time for studying. "It was a school for people much smarter than me," she claimed years later. By the end of her freshman year, the 19-year-old who had held a B average in high school finished with a 1.62 (D-) average. There seemed to be little point in returning the following fall.

But Rosie O'Donnell never gave up that easily. Despite poor grades, she was determined to try college again. This time, she chose Boston University, a much larger school located in the capital of Massachusetts. The university was known for its theater arts department, and Rosie auditioned for the program. She was awarded an acting scholarship after doing the title role from the musical *Hello, Dolly!* (a role that her idol, Barbra Streisand, played on film in 1969).

The sprawling urban campus of Boston University was very different from that of Dickinson. With an enrollment several times greater and a large percentage of students living off campus, the university provided much less structure and supervision than the small-town college Rosie had previously attended.

Sophisticated entertainment was easily accessible, and the aspiring actress took advantage of her location by seeing as many new movies and pre-Broadway shows as she could fit into her schedule. She also frequented the city's comedy clubs to watch others perform. Occasionally she did an engagement herself, and once she even filled in for another, more experienced comic.

This time, only six months passed before Rosie officially ended her college career. Unfortunately, the distractions of the city were not the only reasons she left Boston University. In a theater arts class during her first semester, Rosie was publicly ridiculed by her professor for what she believed was good comic timing. Comparing her to Mary Tyler Moore's sidekick in one of Rosie's all-time favorite sitcoms, *The Mary Tyler Moore Show*, the professor told her that "the part of Rhoda Morgenstern had already been cast and that I would never make it as an actress." At the time, Rosie was humiliated. But the comment, made in front of the rest of her class, strengthened her resolve to forge a career in show business. In a June 1997 interview with *Good Housekeeping* magazine, O'Donnell described her determination as she advised others to believe in themselves:

> If you believe it, you can live it. I know that to be true. . . . Everybody told me, "You won't make it. You're too tough, you're too heavy, you're too this, you're too that." I always thought in my head, "Mmm, no, you're wrong." I wouldn't argue with people; I just believed in myself and kept going. I don't know where I got that, who instilled it in me. But it has definitely guided me through the rocky waters of showbiz.

By the early 1980s, when Rosie O'Donnell began her career as a comic, live stand-up comedy was enjoying a revival. Comedians who previously worked without pay at nightclub gigs were able to demand compensation for their performances.

5

ON THE WAY UP

By 1982, Rosie O'Donnell was a 20-year-old college dropout who was once again living in her father's house on Long Island. With no other job prospects, she set her sights on a full-time career as an actress. But lacking professional credits, contacts, and conventional good looks, Rosie knew she had an uphill struggle ahead of her. What she needed was exposure—and a few lucky breaks. With that in mind, she decided to continue working as a professional comic. Stand-up comedy, she reasoned, might be her best shot at stardom.

O'Donnell was lucky in one sense. The 1980s brought a sharp rise in the popularity of live stand-up comedy in America, and opportunities for up-and-coming comedians were expanding. In his book *Rosie*, James Robert Parish explains that just 20 years earlier, nightclubs hired only established performers for their main acts. They rarely used comics, except to open for singers or other entertainers. Moreover, there were fewer nightclubs to begin with: the advent of television in the 1950s had greatly reduced their numbers by the early 1960s. Only one club in the country—the Improv in Manhattan, New York—showcased new comedic talent at that time, and its husband-and-wife owners, Bud and Silver Friedman, did not pay comics because they considered their club a "training ground" for them.

By the mid-1970s, when the Friedmans divorced and Bud opened a new club, the L.A. Improv, in Los Angeles, California, the original Improv had given rise to such stand-up stars as David Brenner, Bill Cosby, Robert Klein, Freddie Prinze, and Jimmy Walker. The L.A. Improv was successful as well, but it had a direct competitor called the Comedy Store, founded and co-owned by Mitzi Shore. The Comedy Store followed the same policy as the Improv—no pay for comedians—yet among some of its early talents were future stars such as David Letterman, Richard Pryor, and Robin Williams.

In New York, meanwhile, prospects improved for aspiring stand-up comedians. Though neither venue paid its comics, Catch a Rising Star and the Comic Strip became popular as places where talent agents for national TV programs like *The Tonight Show* came to find new acts. This news quickly circulated among up-and-coming comics, and as the number of performing comedians increased, so did the size of the audiences.

In 1979, a group of comics calling themselves "Comedians for Compensation" went on strike at L.A.'s Comedy Store, demanding payment for their work. After a bitter struggle, Mitzi Shore agreed to pay comics a minimum of $25 per set. The L.A. Improv quickly followed suit. And under threat of a similar strike, New York City clubs also agreed to pay their talent.

Though club owners initially feared that this new expense would erode their profits, the comedy business thrived and expanded. Before long, promoters began hiring young comics for "showcase" performances in small bars, dance halls, and other out-of-the-way venues, and the trend spread inward from the East and West Coasts. Around the same time, cable TV networks such as HBO and Showtime discovered that live or

taped stand-up comedy acts provided inexpensive and popular entertainment programs. According to Parish, by 1986 approximately 300 paying showcases had sprung up across the country.

After Rosie O'Donnell decided to do stand-up in 1982, she took a day job at the local Sears department store while she emceed at night in local clubs such as the Eastside Comedy Club, Chuckles, and Governor's. She enrolled in comedy and improvisational acting classes and began doing her own act regularly. She also joined Eastside's improvisational comedy group, the Laughter Company, which became popular around Long Island and developed a sizeable following. Karl Hosch, now a producer, was among the Laughter Company's fans, and he videotaped many of the

Johnny Carson (right), the "king of late-night television," with sidekick Ed McMahon (center) and bandleader Carl "Doc" Severinsen on the set of The Tonight Show. *In the 1980s, New York nightclubs such as the Comic Strip and Catch a Rising Star became "hunting grounds" for talent scouts seeking fresh acts for Carson's popular talk show.*

comics' acts. He clearly remembers the night when he helped Rosie create an audition tape using clips from his own videotapes.

"She said to me, 'You can take it to the bank that I'm going to make it,'" Hosch recalled. "And she said it with such determination that you almost didn't doubt it. You knew that if she didn't make it, she was going to die trying."

O'Donnell quickly earned a reputation in the clubs of Long Island, and she became skilled in developing a network of contacts. She decided to go on the road for more work. With the help of people like Eastside's Rick Messina, she began taking jobs in regional clubs in Buffalo, New York; Trenton, New Jersey; and Wilmington, Delaware. Later, she began traveling what is called the "comedy circuit," which in the early 1980s included clubs in such cities as Boston, Massachusetts; Washington, D.C.; Detroit, Michigan; Cleveland, Ohio; Chicago, Illinois; and San Francisco, California.

Before long, however, she ran into problems with the way her name was announced. Emcees had been introducing her by her given name, Roseann O'Donnell. But the name sounded similar to that of Gilda Radner's popular character Roseanne Rosannadana from *Saturday Night Live*, so some audiences expected to see Radner instead. In one club, O'Donnell was even booed by a crowd who believed that she was trying to imitate Radner. After that, the club's emcee began introducing her as "Rosie," and the nickname stuck. (Years later, when Rosie featured Gilda Radner's brother on her talk show, she laughingly acknowledged that everyone knows her as Rosie because of Radner's wildly popular character.)

Taking a comedy act on the road may sound exciting, but it is usually far from glamorous. Rosie clearly remembered the dreariness of her years as a relatively unknown comedian: "All the comics would share a [club-sponsored] condo. You'd arrive in town and

O'Donnell credits comedian and actress Roseanne Barr with having paved the way for other female stand-up comics during the 1980s.

they'd have a kid come pick you up in a used Vega or Toyota with a door that didn't close. . . . All of us would be scrunched in the back seat, and he'd take us to this filthy condo where we would all live for a few days, with . . . rotten leftover take-out food in the fridge. Very disgusting."

The early '80s may have been the heyday of stand-up comedy, but not for women. Nearly every comedian working the club and college circuits was male. Because of the fierce competition, women comics became resentful of other women who seemed to be succeeding, O'Donnell remembers. But she saw the situation in a different light. "They thought, 'If she gets [a gig on] *The Tonight Show*, I can't.' My philosophy was, 'If she did, we can, too.' Success breeds success."

The Comedy Castle in Detroit, Michigan, the first major club on the comedy circuit where Rosie O'Donnell earned a "headliner" spot.

Female comics also faced discrimination that male comics didn't encounter. One club owner informed O'Donnell that she was only the third woman he'd hired, "and the first two sucked. If you stink, we're not hiring any more [women]." She called the pressure of representing her "entire gender" at that club "horrible." On many other occasions she heard similar comments. "Most women comics suck," another owner told her, "but you were all right."

Rick Haas, the owner of Zanies in Chicago, Illinois, believes that there is an even more fundamental reason why stand-up comedy is more difficult for women: touring can be a dangerous way to make a living. "It isn't that [women are] not funny onstage—it's what goes on offstage," Haas has said. "A guy gets a booking at an out-of-town club. He drives by himself, maybe at night, to this club and parks in the dark parking lot, walks into a strange club, and does his show.

That's hard enough for a guy. For a woman, that [can be] a life-threatening situation."

The few female comics who toured not only had a tougher time becoming successful but were also paid much less than their male colleagues. Rosie had already become a headline act in a number of clubs when she learned inadvertently from one club's female book-keeper that she was being paid less than the male comics appearing there. The bookkeeper thought that someone had made a mistake in the figures—instead of the $1700 payments made to male comics, Rosie was receiving only $700, less than half of that amount.

Characteristically, Rosie O'Donnell has also pointed out the benefits of being one of the few females on the comedy circuit during the 1980s and early 1990s. Because she was seen as an "oddity," she said in 1996, she often attracted more attention from agents than her male counterparts did. "I think that [being a woman] was an asset for me when I started," she said. "I think that if I [were] a male comic . . . it would have taken me a lot longer to . . . get to a certain level."

It wasn't only those in the business who treated female comics differently. Parish notes in his book that the general public's impression of comics as "abrasive, aggressive, [and] sometimes foul-mouthed" does not fit most people's perception of how a woman should behave, either onstage or off. At least one club owner, Wende Curtis of the Comedy Works in Denver, Col-orado, agrees. She believes that it's "something that we all buy into. You'll hear people say, 'She's the funniest woman I've seen.' Well, why isn't she the funniest *comic* you've seen? I'm sure that when Rosie was clear-ing the way for other women, it was tough."

For her part, O'Donnell has steadfastly refused to put other people down to make herself more appealing to audiences. Early in her stand-up career, she decided that she would never say anything about a person dur-ing her act that she wouldn't tell him or her directly.

Making someone laugh, she believes, does not justify being offensive or hurtful.

Instead, Rosie has relied mainly on her own observations of everyday life and on her talent for imitating other people, which once entertained her mother. In that respect, she greatly admires another pioneer of the 1980s: Roseanne Barr, who went on to forge a successful career in television with a sitcom that followed the lives of an average American working-class family. "I think she is a wonderfully funny woman," O'Donnell has said of Roseanne. "She bravely and courageously uses her own life to help other people, and I have nothing but respect for that."

O'Donnell also tries to avoid stereotypical, women-versus-men characterizations in her work. According to Chick Perrin of the Comedy Connection in Indianapolis, Indiana, Rosie "stayed away from the PMS jokes. Audiences would get tired of women comedians doing male-bashing material, but Rosie never did any male bashing. She just told about her life, and it was funny." Comparing her to other comics who came of age during that period, such as Tim Allen, Jeff Foxworthy, and Drew Carey, Perrin says that he realized soon after meeting O'Donnell that she had the skills and talent to be successful. "Rosie had that same type of quality—just really killer shows, every show. You just knew it was a matter of time, and her time would come."

Neither Perrin nor Rosie O'Donnell herself could have predicted how or when her big break would materialize. One night in 1984, after a gig at a Long Island club, Rosie was approached by a woman who asked her whether she was interested in appearing on *Star Search*, a new TV talent contest hosted by Johnny Carson's sidekick, Ed McMahon. Rosie was well aware of what an appearance on this syndicated program would mean. *Star Search* showcased new talent from all over the country, and the competition was fierce. According to George Mair and Anna Green in their book *Rosie*

Rosie O'Donnell and Tim Allen, star of TV's Home Improvement, *performed at some of the same comedy clubs while they were forging their stand-up careers. They met at Detroit's Comedy Castle, where Allen switched places with Rosie in the lineup so that she would have more success with the audience.*

O'Donnell, during that first year on the air, the show's talent scouts sifted through 20,000 auditions of singers, actors, comedians, and other show-business hopefuls to find 160 acts worth presenting on the air.

But Rosie had a hard time believing that the young-looking woman standing before her in that Long Island nightclub was a genuine talent scout. She responded to her question with hardened cynicism: "Oh yeah. Sure," she replied skeptically. Then she found out that the woman was Claudia McMahon, Ed McMahon's daughter.

For a 22-year-old who aspired to become an actress and once imagined herself chatting with Johnny Carson on *The Tonight Show*, going to Hollywood to appear on *Star Search* came pretty close to fulfilling a dream. In her debut appearance, Rosie O'Donnell became the first female contestant to win in the comic category. She kept her title for four more weeks, earning $3,500 each time she beat out another contestant, before losing to another comedian. Including a consolation prize of $1,500, Rosie earned more than $15,000 from her stint on *Star Search*. It was a windfall: to save money during the show's taping, she had been staying in a cheap hotel near the studio, dining mostly on hot dogs she bought from a nearby vendor.

With her prize money, Rosie decided to move to Los Angeles to capitalize on the national exposure she had received. She rented a small apartment, thinking that it would only be a matter of time before movie agents would come calling. What she did not realize, however, was that while *Star Search* was quite popular in other parts of the country, the film industry thought the show was not refined enough to seek talent there.

Disappointed but not defeated, O'Donnell continued doing stand-up in Los Angeles, where her TV appearance had at least given her the clout to begin headlining at a few smaller local clubs. She tried unsuccessfully to break into the elite group of comics regularly featured at the Improv, still the city's most influential club, and continued to travel across the country. Before long she earned the headliner spot at the Comedy Castle in Detroit, Michigan. Each night, the Castle featured three comedians; being headliner meant that Rosie, who received a higher pay, would perform third, since the first two acts were seen as warm-ups for the top comic.

Unfortunately, Rosie's humor didn't go over well in Detroit. "I tanked," she says simply. "When I say tanked, I was horrible. They wouldn't laugh at a thing." She just couldn't connect with the audience. Even worse, the young male comic who was second in the lineup was a local favorite. By the time Rosie got onstage, audiences had already seen his act, and they often greeted O'Donnell with chants of "Tim, Tim, Tim"—the name of the comic whom they'd just heard.

Rosie O'Donnell discussed the situation with the popular comic, and he agreed to switch places in the lineup so that she wouldn't have to follow his act. That way, the two reasoned, O'Donnell would have a better chance at pleasing the crowd. The gesture was more than simple kindness: if Rosie's performance at the Comedy Castle had been canceled, her career could have suffered permanent damage.

The change was exactly what she needed, and it bolstered her confidence during a period when nearly everyone she knew was telling her to give up. "Time and time again people told me to quit, that I was too tough. I was too New York. I was too heavy. But I didn't listen to them," she says. In 1996, Tim Allen, the star of TV's *Home Improvement*—the same comic who had switched places with Rosie in Detroit—appeared as a guest on *The Rosie O'Donnell Show*. Before an audience of millions, Rosie formally thanked Allen for his help years before. "You never asked me for the difference in the money, and you never told any other comics," she said. "[I]t was very nice of you." Allen shot back, "But you owe me eleven hundred dollars now."

After her gig in Detroit, O'Donnell spent another two years on the stand-up circuit. Her diligence began to pay off: she opened for such performers as the illusionist David Copperfield, singer Dolly Parton, and Motown's Temptations, and she appeared in venues such as the Riviera Hotel in Las Vegas, Nevada, and Trump Plaza and TropWorld in Atlantic City, New Jersey.

Back in Los Angeles in 1986, Rosie occasionally

appeared on the same bill with another hardworking comedian named Dana Carvey, who had recently landed recurring roles on two TV series, *One of the Boys* and *Blue Thunder*. One night at Igby's Comedy Cabaret, rumors began circulating that NBC-TV executives would be in the audience to see Carvey's act. Word had it that they were considering him for a regular position on *Saturday Night Live*.

For once, a rumor turned out to be true. Brandon Tartikoff, the director of NBC network programming, and *Saturday Night Live* executive producer Lorne Michaels quickly decided that Carvey would indeed make a great addition to *SNL*'s lineup. They also had a chance to see Rosie O'Donnell.

How did Rosie catch Tartikoff's eye that night? One source claims that the executive saw part of her act while waiting to pay his tab. Another says that not only did Igby's manager ask the executive to stay for O'Donnell's act, but Rosie herself, in the middle of her routine, also pleaded with him to consider her for a TV role. In any event, Tartikoff believed that O'Donnell's tough-girl persona might be perfect for a flagging NBC sitcom called *Gimme a Break*, which had debuted five years earlier.

True to form, Rosie O'Donnell was skeptical when approached by Tartikoff. "I said to myself, 'Yeah, right! Come on. He's not going to do that. That's the kind of story you read in a Hollywood newspaper.'" But Tartikoff meant business. Working with Rosie's agent, NBC officials hammered out a contract that gave her a guest-starring role on one of the new episodes of the 1986-87 season, with the provision that she would become a permanent member of the cast if viewers liked her character.

Gimme a Break had suffered a tremendous loss during its previous season. Soap-opera veteran Dolph Sweet, who played one of the main characters in the show, died of cancer in May 1985 at age 64. Without his presence and the appeal of his character, the show's future was in jeopardy. Having decided not to cancel the series outright, NBC wanted to revamp the show's story line. That's where Rosie O'Donnell and several other new actors came in.

As dental hygienist and upstairs neighbor Maggie O'Brien, Rosie was popular enough to land a regular slot on the show. She was finally earning a decent and steady salary, and she had reached her goal of becoming a TV star, the kind of star that she had watched endlessly as a child. But for *Gimme a Break*, the infusion of fresh characters did little good. The show's original regulars were weary of their roles, and they were haunted by the knowledge that they might soon lose their jobs. As they feared, the program was canceled at the end of the season.

Rosie O'Donnell remembers that event as "the most crushing blow of my career. My goal was to be on a sitcom; then I got on this show in its last year and people weren't ready to be there. I thought, 'I've climbed this mountain and there's nothing there.'"

Despite Rosie's disappointment, she realized that she had come a long way. Her weekly TV role provided the valuable exposure her career needed, and she had made scores of contacts with other actors. She was not about to give up now.

O'Donnell as the host of VH-1's Stand-Up Spotlight.

6

MAKING HER MARK

A lthough Rosie O'Donnell was forced to return to the comedy circuit in 1987 after the cancellation of *Gimme a Break*, she now had a much slicker act, honed by years of hard work, and she had more impressive credentials than ever. Her bookings improved dramatically; not only was she sought after by clubs like the prestigious L.A. Improv, but she also appeared frequently in taped programs for cable channels such as HBO, Showtime, and Arts & Entertainment (A&E).

The following year, Bud Friedman, owner of several nightspots (including the L.A. Improv) and producer of the hour-long A&E program called *An Evening at the Improv*, told Rosie about MTV's search for a veejay (on-camera host) for their music video format. With a television series behind her—and looking for a new direction for her career—Rosie auditioned for the job. Although she didn't make the cut, MTV executives referred her to VH-1, a cable station with a similar music-video format that was also looking for veejays. This time, Rosie was successful. Against the advice of her professional advisors and her fellow comics, many of whom believed that the job would stall her career, Rosie signed a contract to introduce Top 40 rock videos on VH-1 beginning in April 1988.

The job consisted of taping scores of three-minute segments in which the veejay introduces the next block of videos. The taped segments aired seven days a week. The position required someone who was familiar with the network's music and skilled at improvising, someone who could hold viewers' interest during the breaks from the music but not distract from the videos themselves. Rosie O'Donnell, a rock fan and veteran stand-up comedian, fit the bill nicely.

Taking the veejay post meant relocating to the East Coast once again, where VH-1 segments were taped. But by this time, Rosie was ready for a change. Her sister, Maureen, who was married with a daughter, was still living in New Jersey, and Rosie missed Maureen and wanted to spend time with her new niece.

Shortly after O'Donnell started at VH-1, *Newsday* asked her whether she was enjoying herself. "VH-1 is perfect for me right now," she replied. "I get to talk about my life, my weight, Whitney Houston's ego problems, Linda McCartney's off-key singing, my sister's baby, whatever pops into my head." But though she was seen in more than 30 million homes across America, one drawback, she discovered, was that she had to perform without an audience in front of her. "I never know if I'm going over," she explained. "There's a lot of insecurity in a job like this."

To make up for the absence of a live audience, she began to banter with the cameraman, trying to make him laugh and encouraging him to answer her questions by tilting or shaking the camera for "yes" or "no" responses. When producers told her to reintroduce herself for each segment, she developed another gimmick: instead of saying her own name each time, she introduced herself using the name of the first celebrity that came to mind. "Hi, I'm Kiki Dee," she said once, and on another occasion, "Hi, I'm Chaka Khan." The device worked—until the day she introduced herself as Florence Henderson, formerly of *The Brady Bunch*, prompting an angry call from Henderson's manager.

O'Donnell's busy taping schedule did not keep her from doing regular stand-up gigs. Thanks to her TV exposure, she had become a "name" on the circuit, frequently headlining and earning more than ever for her appearances. Around the time she began working for VH-1, she did a set on Showtime's *Comedy Club Network* and then on its *Comedy Club All-Stars* show. The latter, an hour-long special that aired in March 1988, was hosted by comic Harry Anderson of TV's *Night Court*. It featured the best six (out of 92) comics who had appeared the previous year on *Comedy Club Network*. Later that year, she also appeared at New York City's Catch a Rising Star and the Chicago Improv, earning exceptional reviews for both gigs.

In 1989, VH-1, faced with a changing viewership and competing against MTV's greater popularity, decided to replace its veejay format with half-hour specials featuring specific artists such as Anita Baker, Harry Connick Jr., and Melissa Etheridge. Many of the veejays' contracts had not yet expired, and the network was offering to buy them out in an effort to honor their original agreements.

But Rosie O'Donnell thought she had a better idea, and she presented the network's management with a plan. She offered to host a weekly half-hour comedy show featuring two well-known comics and one new talent in each episode. What's more, she told them, she would do the first 20 episodes without pay—provided they began paying her if the program lasted longer than that. After much coaxing and cajoling from O'Donnell, VH-1 agreed to let her host the project and even made her its executive producer. O'Donnell would be responsible for figuring out how to package the test shows.

The new program, *Stand-Up Spotlight*, debuted on Sunday evening, November 19, 1989. It was an imme-

Rather than lose her job when VH-1 eliminated veejays and began highlighting individual artists such as Harry Connick Jr. (shown here), Rosie proposed that the network launch a half-hour comedy program featuring her as its host.

Mark Ridley, owner of Detroit's Comedy Castle, claimed that Rosie treated her Stand-Up Spotlight guests regally. "She's got an incredible work ethic," Ridley said.

diate hit with viewers as well as with the network's management team, who considered its relatively low production cost a bargain. After the first 13 episodes were taped at Rascal's Comedy Club in East Orange, New Jersey, however, VH-1 decided to change venues, moving the program to a long-running club called the Ice House in Pasadena, California. Rosie O'Donnell was on the move again.

Being *Stand-Up Spotlight*'s executive producer meant that O'Donnell not only had to choose her own comics but also had to ensure that they made it to tapings on time and that they were familiar with the show's logistics beforehand. She scheduled backup comics for each episode to avoid the disaster of a last-minute cancellation. And as the show became more popular, she also sifted through thousands of audition tapes from comics across the country who hoped to get their big break on TV.

O'Donnell was well acquainted with the travails of trying to make it big in stand-up comedy. True to her character, she remembered many of her old friends who were fellow comics, and she made every effort to give them a spot on her show. She dispensed with L.A. comedy circuit politics, which dictated that a comic who appeared regularly in one club should not get a spot on a TV showcase taped at another club. "I don't care where you work," Rosie said, "if you're funny, you're on the show."

Once her guests were scheduled, she went out of her way to try and make them feel at ease. Mark Ridley, owner of Detroit's Comedy Castle (where O'Donnell first met Tim Allen), declared that "everybody who did her show told me they were treated like royalty. Even if they didn't get a break from working on the show, they certainly walked away *feeling* like they had just done *The Tonight Show*. She's very sensitive to other comedians coming up through the ranks."

For her part, O'Donnell thoroughly enjoyed her

job as host and executive producer for *Stand-Up Spotlight*. She was gaining tremendous exposure to millions of TV viewers, and she worked with scores of talented comedians whom she considered friends. In addition, she was also able to take a much-needed break from touring the club circuit and trying to land another acting job. "I really enjoy performing," Rosie said then, "but the demands of that lifestyle can take their toll. Producing and writing have shown me there's a lot I can do and still spend more time at home than I do on the road."

Up until this point, Rosie had lived in rented apartments or condos while shuttling from coast to coast. Now she decided to put down roots on the West Coast. She bought a modest two-bedroom house in a quiet, residential area of Studio City in the San Fernando Valley—about 15 minutes by car from West Hollywood.

Stand-Up Spotlight was so successful that it would eventually earn a nomination for an American Comedy Award and a Cable Ace Award. Viacom, the parent company of VH-1 and Showtime, was so pleased with Rosie's accomplishments that it signed her on to perform her own stand-up act in Showtime comedy specials. In addition, *Stand-Up Spotlight* had easily survived the 20-episode trial period Rosie had agreed upon with VH-1's managers, and she was contracted to produce and tape 26 more episodes before the year's end.

By 1990, the stand-up comedy boom that began in the 1980s was still going strong, but its nature had changed somewhat. The clubs that had sprung up across America were now joined by the immensely popular cable TV networks, which viewed comedy shows as an inexpensive means to raise ratings. Comedy specials peppered cable network schedules; it seemed that you could find a stand-up comic on TV almost any time of the day or night. "Comedy is no longer seen as a relief from everyday life, a respite from the stress of workaday activity," one reviewer groused. "Cable TV is turning humor into just another unavoidable part of existence, an unrelenting fact of life from which drama now beckons as a welcome alternative."

But the medium that made stand-up comedy more wildly popular than ever also brought about its eventual decline. Indianapolis club owner Chick Perrin blamed it on Hollywood's tendency to over-market trends until they lose their appeal with audiences. "The very thing that made comedy a hit in the eighties was the thing that killed it in the nineties," he said. "[Hollywood] always kill[s] the golden goose." As the TV market for comics increased, club owners and agents scrambled for new talent. Often, they booked mediocre comics in an effort to fill their schedules, or sent "local" comics—popular in one city or region—to other parts of the country, where their acts didn't "translate."

As a result, paying club customers, realizing that they could see all the free comedy they wanted on television, began staying away. Despite the free tickets and other giveaways many owners resorted to, most comedy clubs began losing money during the 1990s, and many of them closed.

As the comedy club trend faded, comics' salaries dropped. "At the height of the stand-up boom," Jan Maxwell Smith of Igby's said in the early 1990s, "a headliner could make between $2,500 and $3,500 a week. Now, those same people are making $1,500 to $2,000 a week because their competition is gone and there are only a few clubs left, and they're not able to pay eighties prices."

For Rosie O'Donnell—indeed, for any comedian—it was a good time to be on television. O'Donnell was among a small group of comics who, in the early 1990s, realized that writing and producing comedy for TV was more profitable and provided steadier work than performing on the grueling stand-up comedy circuit. Following the lead of comedians like Bill Cosby (*The Cosby Show*) and Roseanne Barr (*Roseanne*), '90s

comics like Tim Allen, Paul Reiser, Ellen DeGeneres, and Jerry Seinfeld parlayed their talents into writing, producing, and acting for television.

Although Rosie loved her job on *Stand-Up Spotlight* and was enjoying great success, she still wanted to be an actor. In 1990, she had finally attained her goal of landing a role in a feature film—but to her great disappointment, the release of the movie, *Car 54, Where Are You?*, was delayed for four years because its distributor, Orion Pictures, was mired in financial problems. (The movie, released in 1994, did poorly at the box office.) Worse yet for Rosie, the experience left her disillusioned. She had difficulty making the transition from live performing, with its immediate audience reaction, to filming, where she was surrounded by technicians who couldn't—and didn't—laugh. Nor could she get used to the tedium of film work. "I

TV personality and film director Penny Marshall with Sesame Street *characters Rosita (left) and Elmo during a K-mart promotion in New York City. Marshall met Rosie in 1991 during an audition for Marshall's film* A League of Their Own; *the two have since become good friends.*

thought . . . I was gonna be working, working, working. Most of it is waiting, waiting, waiting."

Less than a year later, however, Rosie finally got her chance to be a movie star. During the spring of 1991, her agent called to tell her about a casting call for baseball-playing female actors. Penny Marshall, former star of the hit series *Laverne and Shirley* and producer of the movies *Big* (1988) and *Awakenings* (1990), was working on a new movie about the All-American Girls Professional Baseball League, which was founded during World War II to offset the shortage of professional male players, many of whom had been drafted for military duty. (The league was disbanded in 1954.)

Rosie was certain that her time had come when she read the script for *A League of Their Own*. "If there's one thing I can do better than [actresses] Meryl Streep and Glenn Close, it's play baseball," she said. "I started playing baseball when I was five; there were twenty-three boys on my block and six girls—we almost had our own league," she remembered.

The tomboyish veteran of the Commack, New York, neighborhood ball fields had no trouble landing a part—she was cast as Brooklynite Doris Murphy. She laughingly remembered the physical tryouts. "[I]t was really funny to see all these actresses [auditioning] who had never played baseball [and] who had lied to their agents. . . . I'm like, 'Honey, hold the thin end of the bat, OK? Good luck. . . . Be careful out there.'"

Perhaps most amazing to O'Donnell was the fact that she would be working with well-known celebrities such as Tom Hanks, Geena Davis, and Madonna. Rosie remembers that Penny Marshall was anxious to make a good impression on Madonna so that the superstar would be willing to sign on for the part of Doris Murphy's pal, Mae Mordabito. "If she likes you and she likes me, she'll do the movie. Be funny," Marshall commanded O'Donnell. Rosie's childhood dreams were finally blossoming into reality. "When I

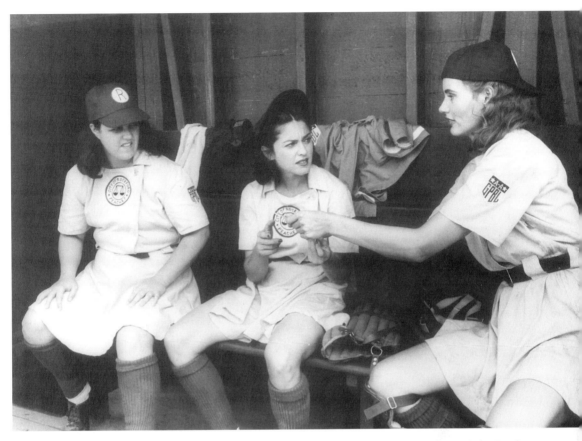

got cast in *League*, I knew something was starting. And when Madonna was cast as my best friend, I thought, 'Well, here we go.'"

Paul Barkley of the Comedy Connection spent some time with O'Donnell the day before she left for Chicago to begin filming *A League of Their Own*. "Boy, tomorrow you go to Chicago to work with Madonna and Penny Marshall—your whole life is going to change," he remembers telling her. "Yeah, I know, it's amazing," Rosie replied.

One of the things the gregarious comic discovered during the movie's filming was that working so closely with other members of the cast and crew made her feel like they were all part of an extended family. During breaks, for example, the cast members took turns

Three members of the Rockford Peaches: Doris Murphy (Rosie O'Donnell), Mae Mordabito (Madonna), and Dottie Hinson (Geena Davis) in the 1992 film A League of Their Own.

entertaining the film's 5,000 unpaid extras, mostly local residents who had volunteered to fill the stadium during taping.

One person with whom O'Donnell grew particularly close was Madonna. Their friendship is now famous, but a shared painful experience brought them together: Madonna was only five when she also lost her mother to cancer. In one version of Rosie's first meeting with Madonna, she introduced herself to the pop star by saying, "My mother died when I was ten, and I totally understand what motivates you."

In interviews, Madonna has explained why she thinks they became quick friends. "Rosie and I speak the language of hurt people," she once said. "She is very protective, loyal, and maternal with me." Rosie herself has described their friendship as "sister-like," and in a July 1993 interview she claimed that the private Madonna is far different from the public's perception of her. "She's not callous at all. . . . She's very sensitive and loving," Rosie maintained.

A League of Their Own premiered in the summer of 1992 and ultimately became a smash hit, earning mostly favorable reviews—and more than $107 million in the United States. It was especially popular with female viewers, who identified with the pioneering sportswomen in the movie. Critic Roger Ebert characterized *A League of Their Own* as a film "about transition—about how it felt as a woman suddenly to have new roles and freedom." Four years after the movie's release, one fan told Rosie, "This movie depicts . . . what I have [only] dreamed about. As a child . . . my dream was to be the first girl Phillies player."

Rosie O'Donnell and Madonna had differing opinions about their experiences with the movie. Not surprisingly, although the summer heat was often unbearable and baseball practice sessions were sometimes tedious, Rosie O'Donnell was thrilled to be involved in a major movie, and she enjoyed the filming. The cosmopolitan Madonna, on the other hand, lost some of her initial enthusiasm once she arrived in the small town of Evansville, Indiana, where most of the filming was done (some scenes were shot at the legendary Wrigley Field in Chicago, where the real Girls League had played some of their games). Madonna was bored and anxious to return to her own home. The residents of Evansville didn't appreciate the star's apparent disdain for the remoteness of the town.

Rosie O'Donnell and Madonna remain great friends, even though their careers and personal lives have taken different directions. They often seek advice from one another. When Rosie was house-hunting in New York in 1996, for example, she took Madonna's advice and looked at the former Helen Hayes estate in Nyack, New York; not long after, she bought the estate. And when Madonna needed advice on setting up a nursery for her first child, Lourdes, born the same year, she turned to Rosie, who had adopted a baby boy in May 1995.

Best friends Betty Rubble (Rosie O'Donnell) and Wilma Flintstone (Elizabeth Perkins) in the movie The Flintstones.

7

A MOVIE STAR

After the success of *A League of Their Own*, Rosie O'Donnell continued to do a few stand-up shows, as well as her usual regular appearances at charity benefits and auctions. But now she was a star, and both the media and her new fans sought her out. Movie audiences loved Doris Murphy, and they wanted to see more of Rosie O'Donnell.

In 1992, the Fox television network offered O'Donnell a role in a new sitcom called *Stand by Your Man*. Starring opposite Melissa Gilbert (the former child star of *Little House on the Prairie*), Rosie played a blue-collar New Jersey woman forced to move into the home of her wealthy sister (Gilbert) after both of their husbands are imprisoned. Unfortunately, the show bombed with viewers, and it was quickly canceled. "[The] Richard Simmons Deal-a-Meal program got higher ratings," Rosie wisecracked.

By now, however, Rosie O'Donnell was busier than ever. Not only had she begun making the rounds of TV talk shows but she was also a presenter for the 1992 prime-time Emmy Awards ceremony, and, a true sign of fame, she appeared as herself on several TV shows, including *Beverly Hills, 90210.*

In the months before *A League of Their Own* was released, Rosie continued to look for more film roles. Among the scripts she received was a sentimental romance by novelist, screenwriter, and director Nora Ephron. Ephron vividly remembers auditioning O'Donnell for a part in the movie *Sleepless in Seattle*. "I had never heard of her," Ephron recalls of her first meeting with Rosie. "I'm unbelievably embarrassed to say that I did not know who she was. She was supposed to stay for ten minutes, and almost an hour later we were still there. The script was in the process of becoming, and after she finished reading what was there, and I went and printed out more that was in the computer, she started talking about her life and her family—it's all right there, amazing."

At dinner that evening, Nora discussed it with her kids. She remembers telling them, "'I saw this woman, I don't know if you've heard of her, she's on VH-1.' And they looked at me like, 'You're even older and more washed up than we've dreamed,' and that was it." Her son urged her to sign on O'Donnell (Rosie still credits him with getting her hired).

In the movie, which stars Tom Hanks and Meg Ryan, Rosie plays Becky, an editor for the *Baltimore Sun* who is a close friend and boss of *Sun* reporter Annie Reed (Ryan). A recently widowed architect named Sam Baldwin (Hanks) moves with his son Jonah (Ross Maliger) to Seattle, where Jonah tries to deal with his father's sadness by calling a radio talk program. The movie's plot revolves around the chance that Annie and Sam, who live on opposite coasts, might ultimately meet and fall in love.

For O'Donnell, whose only film experience was with Penny Marshall, adjusting to Nora Ephron's directing style was difficult at first. While Marshall often allowed the cast to ad-lib their lines, Ephron was exacting. "Nora was insistent that we do [our lines] exactly as written. Verbatim," said Rosie. The director also paid

close attention to the actors' clothing, mannerisms, and speech. Occasionally, out of nervousness, O'Donnell unthinkingly reverted to her normal speaking voice, with its strong New York accent. Ephron would stop her immediately. "You graduated with a master's [degree] from the Columbia School of Journalism," Ephron would remind O'Donnell about her character. "[Y]ou don't speak like you're from the street." In the end, Rosie felt that the experience made her a better actor. Being "molded" in that way, she later commented, "was difficult . . . in a good way, in a challenging way. There was no room to be lazy."

Sleepless in Seattle earned $17 million in the first weekend it was released in June 1993, and it ultimately grossed more than $126 million at the box office and more than $65 million in videotape rental

A scene from the 1993 movie Sleepless in Seattle, *which featured Rosie O'Donnell as Becky and Meg Ryan (right) as Annie. Rosie characterized her role in the movie as the "sassy best friend with a heart of gold."*

fees. More important for Rosie, she received her first nomination for an acting award from the American Comedy Awards.

During her first few years as a film star, Rosie was concerned about being characterized as a big-mouthed tomboy like Doris Murphy in *A League of Their Own*. But in all the movies she has done since, the only typecasting Rosie has encountered has been that of the best friend or sidekick—and she doesn't have a problem with that. After *Sleepless in Seattle* was released, Rosie described her type of film character as the "sassy best friend with a heart of gold" or the "second banana who's got all the funny lines." Besides, she pointed out, she played best-friend roles with some impressive actresses. "In my first movie, I'm best friends with Madonna; my second, I'm best friends with Meg Ryan," Rosie said. "That's not a bad career right there."

A realist at heart, O'Donnell knows that she is not a classically trained actress and doesn't wish to be one. "I have no aspirations to do Shakespeare," she maintains. "This is exactly what I'm equipped to do and what I like to do." O'Donnell's friend Kate Capshaw agrees, comparing O'Donnell to actress Shelley Winters, who played tough but vulnerable characters in the 1950s. "They both have that strength of body and face, yet you always feel that bareness, that fragility under-neath," Capshaw said in 1996.

Curiously, Rosie O'Donnell never set foot in Seattle, Washington, until after *Sleepless in Seattle* was complet-ed. To avoid the expense of flying an entire cast and crew to an offsite location for filming, most studios film as much as possible on studio sound stages or back lots. Such was the case with O'Donnell's scenes in *Sleepless in Seattle*. Not until she began work on the action-comedy film *Another Stakeout* (a 1993 sequel to the 1987 film *Stakeout*) did she get a glimpse of the north-western city. Although set in Seattle, *Another Stakeout*

was primarily filmed in Canada—in Vancouver, British Columbia, not far from Seattle.

O'Donnell was cast as Assistant District Attorney Gina Garrett, who is assigned to supervise two police detectives on a surveillance detail. She later admitted that she had told a fib or two in her eagerness to land a part in the movie. "They said to me, 'Can you drive a souped-up stunt car?' and I said, 'I've had a souped-up stunt car for *years!*' I didn't even know how to drive a stick shift at the time."

Making this movie was another pleasant experience for Rosie. As with *A League of Their Own*, O'Donnell and her costars, Richard Dreyfuss and Emilio Estevez, improvised a great deal, and she enjoyed working with both actors. Dreyfuss, whose acting style Rosie characterized as "very over-the-top and big," encouraged her to go all out with her character. "I'm glad he did," she said, "because those times ended up being the funny

Detectives Bill Reimers (Emilio Estevez) and Chris Lecce (Richard Dreyfuss) team up with lawyer Gina Garrett (O'Donnell) and a canine companion in the 1993 film Another Stakeout.

parts of the film." She added, "Richard is the nicest and smartest guy I have ever worked with. He is a dedicated dad and a remarkable friend."

O'Donnell is equally enthusiastic about Emilio Estevez, calling him her favorite actor. "I adore him, and we have the same strange sense of humor. We laughed the whole time." Perhaps they laughed too much—reportedly, their antics ruined quite a few takes and exasperated director John Badham. Estevez named O'Donnell as the instigator. "If I looked at Rosie," he said, "I was just gone. Same with Richard. The director wasn't happy, but we had a good time."

The actors may have enjoyed themselves, but the movie was a box-office disappointment. Rosie O'Donnell received mixed reviews: one critic called her acting "drab," but others praised her for adding life to an otherwise predictable movie. Abbie Bernstein of *Drama-Logue* called her "a force to be reckoned with. . . . Almost absurdly emotional yet wonderfully sharp and bulldog-stubborn, Gina as played by O'Donnell is a splendidly comic figure who remains in the memory after the film concludes."

O'Donnell's next two film roles were minor. The first was in *Fatal Instinct* (1993), an attempt to spoof "serious" thrillers that deal with the consequences of adultery, such as *Basic Instinct* and *Fatal Attraction*. Rosie O'Donnell has one brief scene with the star, Armand Assante. The second, *I'll Do Anything* (1994), a comedy originally conceived as a musical, starred Nick Nolte as a self-absorbed actor forced to care for his young daughter. In one memorable scene, O'Donnell is a makeup artist who is sent away by Nolte, who claims he needs to "focus." As Rosie exits, she quips to another character, "Have you seen the pastry truck? Has that guy been by yet? Let's focus on a Danish."

In the spring of 1993, Rosie O'Donnell's agent called her about another upcoming film project. Stephen Spielberg's Amblin Entertainment production

company was working on a movie version of the popular 1960s animated cartoon series *The Flintstones* for
Universal Pictures. They were interested in having
Rosie read for the part of Betty Rubble, the best friend
of Fred Flintstone's wife, Wilma.

Rosie remembers having a good laugh over that. "I
thought, are you kidding me? [Betty] is this tiny little
petite thing, and I'm not exactly similar to the cartoon
rendering. . . . Then when I went in and read it and
everyone laughed, I thought, OK." As it turned out,
the director's wife had met Rosie at a charity function
and suggested her for the part.

Those years of TV-watching paid off: Rosie believes
that her faithful impression of Betty Rubble's unique
laugh landed her the part. The casting people, she said,
"asked what this giggle was from. I said, 'Betty does
that after every line; watch the show.'" Even the director, Brian Levant, was amazed at O'Donnell's knowledge of trivia from the original show. "I was embarrassed," he said about his initial meeting with her. "She
even knew the words to 'The Twitch,' the song from
the 1963 series opener."

The Flintstones, released in May 1994, was harshly
reviewed by critics, but it was a huge hit with audiences,
who viewed it as the perfect family picture, a movie that
entertained nostalgic parents as well as their children.
Within three days of its premiere, it grossed $37.2 mil-
lion in the United States alone. Three months later, the
worldwide take was more than $225 million.

Rosie O'Donnell's appearance in *The Flintstones*
transformed her popular image. Already familiar to
adults and older teens who knew her from *Stand-Up
Spotlight* and her appearances in other films, Rosie now
became wildly popular among pre-teens and young
children. And that was just fine with her. Although she
wasn't nominated for an American Comedy Award as
expected, she would earn the 1995 Kids Choice Award
for Favorite Movie Actress—an honor determined by

Perfect hostess Betty Rubble (O'Donnell), with husband Barney (Rick Moranis) in The Flintstones. *Like her character in the 1994 movie, Rosie adopted a baby boy in 1995.*

26 million Nickelodeon TV viewers.

Rosie was thrilled. "Of all the awards that I've ever been nominated for or received," she said some time later, "the one that's most important is that one." Although she usually donates her trophies to charity auctions, she has held on to the blimp-shaped Nickelodeon award. "I can't really explain the appeal I have to children," she says, "but I know that I adore them and it's a mutual admiration club."

While Rosie O'Donnell took on more film roles, she continued to stay involved in stand-up comedy. She was still the executive producer of *Stand-Up Spotlight*, which was running strong, but she had given her role as on-camera host to a fellow Long Islander named Bobby Collins, who had also traveled the stand-up circuits and had done a few minor acting gigs. "It's really been a great experience for me," Rosie maintained about *Stand-Up Spotlight*. The job had provided a wealth of behind-the-scenes experience, and as executive producer she would continue with one of her favorite assignments: "finding young talent[s] who haven't done TV."

In 1993, Rosie realized another dream: she became a host on *Saturday Night Live*. At times, she had difficulty believing the magnitude of her own fame. Some time after her November 13 appearance, she said, "I'll be watching *Saturday Night Live* and think, 'Gee, I wish I could host that show,' then I'd realize, 'Oh yeah, I did!'"

At the same time, Rosie stayed heavily involved in fund-raising for various causes. The year before her *SNL* debut, she taped a segment for Showtime's "Hurricane Relief" special organized by pop singer Gloria Estefan to benefit Florida disaster victims. She also appeared on the game show *Jeopardy* as one of the celebrities who donated their winnings to charity. In 1993, Rosie appeared in a 30-hour "Laugh-athon" at the L.A. Improv to aid Midwest flood victims, and in Santa Monica she emceed with Gloria Steinem in a benefit for Voters for Choice.

Meanwhile, if O'Donnell had any lingering concerns about being typecast in films, her next role would put them to rest. In *Exit to Eden*, she would play a Los Angeles detective named Sheila Kingston who goes undercover to track diamond smugglers at a remote island resort designed for sexual adventures.

Rosie says that she took the part because of the film's director, Garry Marshall, whom she met while filming *A League of Their Own* with his sister, Penny. Garry Marshall approached her after Sharon Stone rejected the role. Rosie was highly amused. "I was hysterical laughing on the phone," she remembers. "I couldn't imagine that meeting where they say, you know, 'Can't get Mel Gibson, let's get Danny DeVito.' You know, it didn't make sense to me that they would go from Sharon Stone to me. So I took the gig just on that premise alone." (She would later admit that there were other incentives, such as filming on location in Hawaii and working with one of her favorite actors, Dan Aykroyd of *Saturday Night Live* and the movies *Ghostbusters* and *The Blues Brothers.*)

But Marshall had good reasons for choosing O'Donnell over other, more glamorous stars. After Stone turned down the part, he realized that the subject matter of *Exit to Eden*, which was based on Anne Rice's novel of the same name, would be better received by mainstream audiences if it were presented with a healthy dose of humor. He believed that Rosie would be best at "mixing the comic with the erotic. We were trying something very new, and we needed someone with whom the audience could identify to ease them into this slightly kinky, slightly threatening world," he said. Although Rosie's character provides many of the film's funniest moments, "she's still sexy," says Marshall, "and for the first time in her career, [Rosie] . . . has a romantic thing going."

In the movie, Rosie has to dress and act like other vacationers on the resort island where she and her partner, Fred Lavery (Aykroyd), have tracked the smugglers (played by Stuart Wilson and supermodel Iman). At first, Rosie was intimidated by the skimpy costumes she had to wear for some scenes. But she decided that she would use the opportunity as a way to come to terms with her own self-image. Comparing the costumes to one-piece bathing suits, Rosie told a *Los Angeles Times* interviewer, "I have enough problems wearing a one-piece bathing suit at family parties, never mind in front of all America in a film. So I took it [as] a way to get over my own problems about my body image and to try to face the things that I fear."

Perhaps for this reason, O'Donnell appreciated Marshall's ability to create a "family atmosphere" on what

O'Donnell at the October 1994 premiere of Exit to Eden, *displaying a typical costume worn by her character, Sheila. Initially apprehensive about wearing skimpy costumes, Rosie used the experience to overcome her own fears and doubts about her physical appearance.*

might otherwise have been an uncomfortable set. For example, she was surprised to discover that the extra hired to watch her perform an exotic dance in the opening scene was actually Garry Marshall's dentist. "That's the people he casts in the film!" she said with delight. "His hairdresser, his mother's friend from Brooklyn, whatever."

Unfortunately, the film was ultimately a failure. During test screenings, audiences had objected to some of the movie's more explicit scenes, so they had been cut and replaced with light comedy scenes for the movie's release. Marshall also added a voice-over narrative by Sheila, Rosie's character. The result struck critics—and audiences—as uneven and inconsistent. It was "an unmitigated critical bomb," according to *Newsday*. "*Exit to Eden* is a mess," the *New York Times* complained, "a movie that changes gears so often and so nonsensically it seems to have been edited in a blender." Rosie O'Donnell, however, was reviewed more favorably. In the same column, the *Times* praised her down-to-earth performance. "[S]he delivers enough wisecracks and voice-over witticisms to paper over the movie's worst embarrassments."

Early on, however, O'Donnell learned not to take herself—or her critics—too seriously. "If you start believing [them], you change who you are, and you start performing for them. You start thinking, 'Let me be good for the reviewer,' instead of the audience. I think that's the downfall of a lot of artists."

O'Donnell herself did not mince words when describing *Exit to Eden*. "I'd like to refund your money if you did see it," she told online fans two years later in 1996. "It was the most fun I ever had and by far the worst film I've ever made and probably the worst I've ever seen."

Rosie O'Donnell now had seven movie roles, two short-lived TV series, and a stand-up comedy TV show under her belt. She had lived in California for four years, and she was beginning to feel unbalanced there. Living so close to the film industry's capital, Rosie found it nearly impossible to distance herself from work and find time for a private life. "[Y]our whole life is centered around show business," Rosie reflected, "and the more successful you become in it, the harder it is to get away from it." For the 32-year-old comedian and actress, it was time to move closer to her roots. And in doing so, she would fulfill her biggest childhood dream, one that would have made Roseann O'Donnell proud. She would perform on Broadway.

The star of her own show: Rosie in a promotional photo for The Rosie O'Donnell Show.

8

BROADWAY AND MOTHERHOOD

lthough by the mid-1990s Rosie O'Donnell's film career had made her a household name, she felt restless not only in her personal life but also professionally. Since the days when she sat in the balcony of Radio City Music Hall with her mother, she had never shaken her desire to perform in a Broadway musical. "To me, there is nothing like the thrill of going to a Broadway show, when the lights go down and you have that orchestra in front of you. I always get goosebumps," she said. "It's the reason I went into show business in the first place."

While O'Donnell was filming *The Flintstones* in California, she learned that the acclaimed choreographer and director Tommy Tune was planning to revive the 1970s musical *Grease!* on Broadway. (The stage version was made into a successful movie starring John Travolta and Olivia Newton-John in 1978 and was rereleased in 1998.) Rosie was especially drawn to the character of Betty Rizzo, the toughest member of Rydell High's Pink Ladies gang. This, Rosie thought, would be her chance to turn a fantasy into reality.

But her agent, Risa Shapiro, was against the idea of her auditioning. "More people see you in one movie than will ever see you in a two-year run of a Broadway show," she reminded O'Donnell. Most of Rosie's friends agreed. Many also thought it was a risky career move, pointing out that she had no experience whatsoever in theater—a far different venue from film—and that the financial rewards of moviemaking were far greater. Tom Hanks warned her that the experience would be boring rather than exciting. Even her therapist, Rosie joked, counseled her against it.

Rosie O'Donnell was determined, however, and she had answers for all of them. She knew her limits—she was not suited for most Broadway roles, and she had only a passable singing voice—but Rosie also knew that she could succeed if she worked hard enough:

> As a performer and an artist, I want to stretch myself to do things that I thought I couldn't or that other people didn't expect me to do. . . . The film career is always going to be there. Some people don't understand why I'd do this now, but everyone makes their own choices. There's not one road map to follow that automatically lands you at success. You have to cut your own way through the jungle.

As for the money, Rosie explained in 1994 that the lure of earning huge sums in Hollywood was precisely one of the reasons she wanted to try something different. "I did three movies in a row," she told an interviewer, "and if you're a comedic actor you get into a niche in everybody's mind. And then when you're hot, you end up doing a lotta bad movies . . . 'cause they offer you so much money." She added, "I thought taking *Grease!* for a year would remove any chance for me to do that."

In June 1993, Rosie flew to New York to promote the release of *Sleepless in Seattle*—and to audition for the part of Rizzo in *Grease!* With her usual candor and enthusiasm, Rosie not only auditioned for the part but also "sold" herself to the show's casting team. Describing her roles in films like *A League of Their Own, Sleepless in Seattle,* and *The Flintstones,* which was scheduled to open at the same time as the musical, Rosie assured them that adding her name to the bill would help sell tickets.

In the end, she won them over despite her lack of theater credentials, and she signed a 10-month contract during which the cast would rehearse, take the musical on the road, and then return to New York to premiere on Broadway in May 1994.

The punishing rehearsal schedule was an eye-opener for O'Donnell. Unlike moviemaking, where an actor often spends most of her time waiting for her next scene, stage rehearsals can be arduous. "There's a five-minute break every hour, and that's it," Rosie observed. "And if you're not singing or dancing, you're learning your lines . . . or going over your vocal part with the musical director. It's very grueling." A veteran of the comedy circuit, she was also surprised by the physical demands of taking a musical on the road. The difference, she discovered quickly, was that she wasn't alone onstage. "As a stand-up comic, you only have yourself to answer to. You don't have 23 other members of the cast to think about." When filming a movie, a mistake can be corrected with a simple retake, but Rosie was performing live, with other cast members relying on her.

Far from feeling superior to the stage actors with whom she worked, Rosie admired their talent and professionalism. Her own inexperience made the job even more challenging. She had to work on her singing with a voice coach, and although she'd claimed in her audition that she knew how to dance, she had greatly exaggerated. In both cases, the cast and crew offered advice and support whenever necessary. Even the director, Jeff Calhoun, who believed that O'Donnell "could be a very good singer with the proper training," arranged Rizzo's two solo numbers so that other singers joined in on the final bars to add strength to Rosie's untrained voice.

A dream come true: O'Donnell (left) joins other cast members as they rehearse for the Broadway opening of Grease! *in 1994.*

As time went on, however, O'Donnell realized that although she was enjoying the experience of performing onstage, she didn't agree with the message of *Grease!* After her contract expired, she remarked that she thought some of the lines in the musical were "quite sexist, very homophobic, very racist." The musical also seemed to be telling people—especially young girls—that one had to transform oneself from "a nice, normal girl" into a "trampy" girl to win acceptance. At times, Rosie wanted to tell her audience "Don't believe it!"

Two elements of the theater experience made it all worthwhile for Rosie O'Donnell. For one, she was now back on the East Coast, where most of her family and friends lived and where she would have more time to herself. She also loved the thrill of appearing onstage, especially when children were in the audience.

In particular, O'Donnell derived great joy from seeing parents and kids lining up outside the stage door after a show to see the stars emerge, just as she had done with her mother more than 20 years before. "*That's* why you do it!" she declared during the tour. And Roseann O'Donnell was never far from her daughter's mind. At curtain call on opening night, with her family in the audience, Rosie announced in an emotional speech that her great regret was that her mother wasn't there to see her.

Rosie's performance earned mixed reviews. Many cited her lack of experience in theater; others delivered harsh critiques of her acting and singing skills. "Rosie O'Donnell . . . barely makes an impression," said one reviewer. The *New Yorker* conceded that, while Rosie didn't have the finest singing voice, she seemed "so happy to be part of this enterprise that . . . you're on her side." Some critics delivered high praise. "Her sardonic humor suits the role and she, more than any other actor, gives her character a little extra dimension," said *Drama-Logue*.

By the time her contract expired in the fall of 1994, Rosie O'Donnell was ready to admit that a career on the stage was not for her. But that fact didn't bother her—after all, she had finally achieved what she'd dreamed of as a child, and that was more than enough to convince her that she had made the right decision after all.

By the end of 1994, Rosie O'Donnell seemed to be everywhere: in movies like *The Flintstones* and *Exit to Eden*, on Broadway in *Grease!*, on television programs such as *Late Night with David Letterman* (the first of several appearances was in January 1994), and even in the answer to a *Wheel of Fortune* puzzle (Rosie herself popped out from behind the game show's scenery just as one of the contestants solved the puzzle). In November, she returned to the big screen. This time, she traveled to Savannah, Georgia, to appear as hometown doctor Roberta Martin in a New Line movie called *Now and Then*, a nostalgic story about four women who reunite in the town where they grew up when one of them gives birth to her first child.

Rosie was excited about the new project, not only because she had the opportunity to work with her good friend Rita Wilson (the wife of another friend, Tom Hanks) but also because she was appearing opposite stars such as Melanie Griffith and Demi Moore. She also liked the fact that the movie was being produced and directed by women and that its plot concerned friendships between girls, a subject not often covered by Hollywood. Since her role was relatively small, Rosie had plenty of time to observe the process of filmmaking, which she hoped to try herself at some point.

Now and Then premiered in October 1994 and was fairly successful with viewers, but it received lukewarm reviews. Although some critics hailed it as a sweet coming-of-age tale, others called it artificial and forced. One of the problems, it turned out, was that the movie had been promoted using the four adult stars, Moore, Griffith, Wilson, and O'Donnell, who actually had less screen time than the actors who played their characters as youngsters.

Rosie O'Donnell's affinity for children showed not only in her role as Roberta Martin but also on the set of the movie itself. Although she enjoyed the company of her adult costars while filming *Now and Then*, she also spent hours with the young actors hired to play the four friends when they were children. One of them, Gaby Hoffman, she already knew from *Sleepless in Seattle*.

It may have been pure coincidence that the previous year in *The Flintstones*, Rosie O'Donnell had played Betty Rubble, the mother of an adopted child. But in 1995 her personal life would mirror that of her fictional character: she decided to adopt a baby.

As with her stint on Broadway, her decision may have stunned her fans, but those who knew Rosie were not surprised. She had given the idea a great deal of

thought. "I always knew I would have children," she told Liz Smith in a 1997 interview for *Good House-keeping* magazine. "It was never a question. Just as I knew what I wanted for my career, I knew I would be a mother. And though I was not against being a birth mother, this opportunity came up. . . . I put myself on a list, like throwing a wish into the air. I thought, 'If this is meant to be, then it will happen.'"

Rosie held few illusions about what life would be like with a child. She had spent enough time with her brothers' and sister's children to be aware of the realities of motherhood; in fact, she considered her nieces one of her priorities and often tried to arrange her calendar around their activities. More than that, she had spent much of her adolescence as a surrogate mother to her siblings after their own mother died. And though

Childhood friends Roberta Martin (O'Donnell), Chrissy Dewitt (Rita Wilson), and Samantha Albertson (Demi Moore) in Now and Then, *1995. The film also starred Melanie Griffith as Tina Tercell.*

"I always knew I'd have children in my life," Rosie has said. "It was a given for me." Here, mother and son, Parker Jaren, attend a WNBA game in July 1997.

she knew it would be difficult to maintain her hectic work schedule while raising a child, she also knew that she wanted more for herself than stardom. She explained this in a TV interview in early 1995: "[M]y four-year-old niece looked up at me [one day] and said, 'Aunt Ro, work, work, work' because I was on the phone and she wanted me to play. And it broke my heart and I thought, you know, 'You've got to really change your direction.' . . . I figured I'd be 50 years old with awards. . . . But on Christmas morning they don't mean very much, you know?"

Rosie was fortunate to have made her decision during a time when the show business industry had grown increasingly accommodating for women who wanted to raise children and continue to work. Former talent agent Joan Hyler observes that in recent years, Hollywood has become "very family-friendly," perhaps because many actresses, such as Michelle Pfeiffer, Jodie Foster, Diane Keaton, and Amanda Bearse, have chosen to become single mothers. Television and film studios must adapt to the schedules and demands of celebrity mothers, or they lose the opportunity to sign them on for their projects.

For Rosie, having a child meant that she first had to decide whether to adopt or to undergo artificial insemination, since she had no romantic interest in her life. Ultimately, she chose to adopt. She made no attempt to hide the fact that her celebrity status made the usually arduous process easier and faster. In an interview with NBC-TV's Katie Couric, she admitted, "The truth is, having money helps in every situation. . . . the money that comes with stardom makes life easier in [many] way[s], I can't deny that." And anyway, Rosie said, "I think you get the child you're supposed to have in your life." She also hoped that, by talking openly about her own experience, she would encourage others to give some thought to providing a good home for children in need of families.

The child whom Rosie O'Donnell would adopt was born prematurely on May 25, 1995, in Florida. Just a few hours later, Rosie's lawyer had a photo of the infant delivered to her. The new mom immediately called her sister, Maureen, with the news. "My son is a smushed-up tomato, all red and blotchy!" Rosie told her. Maureen replied that it was normal for newborns to look that way. "Now," says Rosie, "I think he's the most gorgeous child I've ever seen."

Rosie named her son Parker Jaren. Although a year later she joked with actress Kirstie Alley that she had named him after Alley's ex-husband, actor Parker Stevenson, she has also said that she simply wanted the boy to have a name "that would work if he were a

Actress Kate Capshaw with her husband, filmmaker Stephen Spielberg. Capshaw was an invaluable source of advice and comfort for Rosie as she adapted to motherhood in 1995.

surfer or a Supreme Court judge." Parker's middle name came from his mother's desire to carry on the family tradition of giving male children the middle initial *J* (she and her siblings had called their brother Timmy "T. J." as a child). Like any mother, though, O'Donnell has her share of affectionate nicknames for Parker, including "Boo Bear."

Despite her experience with children, Rosie was a very nervous new mother. She was grateful for the advice and guidance she received from Rita Wilson and Kate Capshaw, actress friends who were already mothers. She remembers one instance when she was having trouble feeding Parker, and Wilson brought her own mother to reassure her. "To me, he was this tiny little boy. He wouldn't eat. I was so scared. But Rita's mother got him to drink a whole bottle." As for Capshaw, Rosie says, "During the first three months [after Parker's birth] I thought she should establish 1-800-CALL-KATE for new mothers."

Rosie has received child-rearing advice and encouragement not only from friends and family but also from her fans. One woman, who is also a single mother, sent her the following letter via E-mail: "Being a single parent has been the greatest. My kid's life won't be perfect, but it won't be any different than a kid with two parents. Go for it!" Another woman, who was herself an adopted child, wrote, "My son's name is also Parker, and he is adopted—but I am the birth mom. I and other birth mothers are SO thankful for people like you. I love my son more than life itself, and I found someone who can take better care of him than I could. Good luck in all that you do; I am a big fan!"

O'Donnell has also noticed that many women, including fans, react to her differently now that she is a mother. Often, she is approached in public not because she is a celebrity but because she is a parent. "I'm able to connect with people on an innate maternal level. My fame has been superseded by my parenting, which I love," she observes, adding drolly, "I'm in the sorority now."

Until Parker was born, every Mother's Day was a sad reminder of the parent Rosie O'Donnell had lost. But in 1996, just a few weeks before Parker's first birthday, Rosie found herself celebrating the occasion for the first time since her childhood. For once, she told *Good Housekeeping* in 1997, "it was not painful. For the first time I felt sort of celebratory. I felt joy instead of dread and loneliness."

With Rosie's newfound happiness came a greater understanding of her own mother. Because Roseann

O'Donnell died when Rosie was very young, she had grown up with a child's idealized view of her parent. Now that she had her own son, she was able to perceive her mother as an adult, a woman much like herself. She recalled:

> When I first held my son in my arms, I had that overwhelming connection and a feeling of immense love that I never had before. I thought, "My mother felt this for me. And for my siblings." So it was a really emotional time for me, those first few months with Parker, to connect with my mom and to think of her as a woman and not as my little girl's image of her.

Another aspect of having lost her mother while she was a child was Rosie's underlying pessimism about her own life. She had struggled with the belief that she would die young, just as her mother had. But adopting a child gave her a new outlook—and the conviction that she would live a long life and see Parker grow up. "It's like you grow another heart," she said, "like someone kicks down a door that was sealed shut, and then the whole world—sunshine, flowers—falls through."

To those who view her decision to become a single parent as being unfair to her child, she says, "This baby would have been raised in a single-parent household had he been kept by the birth family. There are many different structures that make up a family—and we're definitely a family." Moreover, Rosie believes that her three brothers, whom she sees regularly, serve quite well as male role models for her children. In fact, she believes that becoming a mother has made her feel closer to her siblings, especially her sister, Maureen.

In an interview with *People* magazine, Rosie said that becoming a parent immediately changed her priorities. While still working, she had to adapt to the long and irregular hours that are part of caring for an infant, and she realized that her home life came first. What she wanted most was to give her child a home in which he would grow up safe, not only physically but also emotionally—a feeling she didn't have after her mother's death. "You know, the world can always be unsafe, but your home has to be a safe place," she declared in 1996. "[Parker] has a safe, loving home where he's known, accepted, appreciated, and loved." And that, to Rosie O'Donnell, is the best that anyone can give a child.

Rosie O'Donnell proudly displays her Emmy Award for Outstanding Talk Show Host in May 1997. The following year, Rosie won three Emmys, sharing the Outstanding Talk Show Host award with Oprah Winfrey.

9

FAME

While adjusting to the joys and demands of motherhood, Rosie O'Donnell continued to work full-time. In 1995 she took a minor role in another movie, *Beautiful Girls*, a story of a New York City musician who returns to his small-town home for his 10-year high school reunion and discovers that his old friends—and the town—haven't changed at all. In a role similar to the one she played in *Now and Then*, Rosie starred as Gina Barrisano, the wisecracking, unmarried owner of a local beauty parlor in Knight's Ridge, Massachusetts.

Beautiful Girls was a box-office disappointment, but once again, O'Donnell was a critical success. "The link holding this amazing cast together," wrote Joe Baltake of the *Sacramento Bee*, "is Rosie O'Donnell, who . . . serves as Greek chorus and voice of reason. Her response to things: 'Get on with it.'" A few reviewers even complained that Rosie's talent was underused. Manohla Dargis of the *Los Angeles Weekly* wrote that Gina was "funny, but not consequential" because the movie portrayed her as being below the standards of beauty that it attempted to parody. "Gina stays a joke, a woman alone whose indignation is ulti-

O'Donnell as Ole Golly with Michelle Trachtenberg in the movie Harriet the Spy *(1996). Rosie's love of children was evident during the movie's filming; she delighted in giving her young costars "shoulder rides" and engaging in thumb-wrestling competitions with them.*

mately answered by ridicule," Dargis wrote.

Around the time that Rosie was going through the process of adopting Parker, she was also preparing to make a big return to stand-up comedy. While performing at an AIDS fund-raiser in 1994, she realized that she had been out of practice for so long that she couldn't remember some of her lines. To get her act back into shape in time for her first *HBO Comedy Hour* special, which would air in April 1995, O'Donnell hit the road again and headed for Boston. She later took her new act to Atlantic City, New Jersey, and then on to Las Vegas, Reno, and Lake Tahoe, Nevada.

After a few uneven performances, O'Donnell was back in form again. But she realized immediately that she had to revamp her act. After all, her life had changed drastically—she was now a movie star—and audiences would expect to hear about what her life was like and how she had adjusted to fame. "The thing is," she said at the time, "when you get rich and famous, you're no longer like your average audience member. They have a perception of me that I'm different from them. When I go to McDonald's, people go, 'What are you doing here?'"

By this time, Rosie O'Donnell was in greater demand than ever, not only for movie roles, but also for television sitcoms, stand-up acts, and charity fundraisers. In March 1994, she made one of her most thrilling television appearances: she was a presenter at the 66th Annual Academy Awards ceremony. "Look at me," she exclaimed when she took the podium. "I'm on the Academy Awards. Can you believe it?" She appeared on the awards show the following year as part of a taped "audition" sketch in which celebrities vied for David Letterman's one-line role in the movie *Cabin Boy*. In 1995, she was also a presenter for Nickelodeon's Eighth Annual Kids' Choice Awards—and won one herself. In 1996, she cohosted the event and appeared again on *Saturday Night Live*. Around that time she also began filming commercials with her pal Penny Marshall for the K-mart store chain; the popular spots are still running.

That same year, Rosie played Oscar the Grouch's "Fairy Grouchmother" on a *Muppets Tonight* TV segment, and she was a guest on *Late Night with David Letterman*. She also played herself in a cameo appearance in the movie *A Very Brady Sequel*. In September 1996, she was a presenter at the MTV Video Music Awards as well. A month later, Rosie O'Donnell beat out stars such as Gillian Anderson, Sandra Bullock, Teri Hatcher, and Meg Ryan to win *People Magazine Online*'s first Icon Award for most popular female entertainment figure. Perhaps most significantly, in 1995 Rosie received her first Emmy Award nomination for Outstanding Individual Performance in a Variety or Music Program for her *HBO Comedy Hour* Special. Another nomination came in 1996 for her guest appearance on an episode of the *Larry Sanders Show*.

In 1996, Rosie added another film role to her resumé, playing Ole Golly the nanny in an adaptation of Louise Fitzhugh's novel *Harriet the Spy*. As a child, Rosie had loved the book and had read it over and over. "It encourages young girls to be independent and artistic and intellectual and strong," she said. She also hoped that by appearing in a movie aimed at a young audience, she could soften her image as a brassy, smart-talking character.

As with *Now and Then*, Rosie had great fun working with young cast members on the set of *Harriet the Spy*. Her costar, Michelle Trachtenburg, who was 11 at the time, described a "cherry-pit spitting" competition Rosie instigated one day. "I'd much prefer to do movies with kids than adults because . . . they'll have cherry pit fights with you, which Demi Moore won't do," Rosie said after filming was completed. "You know, you spit on a kid, they like you for life." Audiences enjoyed the movie despite its mostly unfavorable reviews.

During that same period, O'Donnell also had a cameo (brief) role as a nun named Sister Terry in another feature film, *Wide Awake* (1998), the story of 10-year-old boy dealing with his grandfather's death. She also accepted a part in a made-for-TV movie called *The Twilight of the Golds*, based on the 1993 Broadway play of the same name.

While on location in Toronto, Ontario, to film *Harriet the Spy*, Rosie realized that pursuing a full-time career as an actress would prevent her from being the hands-on mother she wanted to be. Although she had taken Parker along with her to Canada, the long hours on the set left little time to spend with him. Remembering how she had felt forsaken by her own father, Rosie began considering other career paths that would allow her to keep a more regular schedule and spend more time with Parker.

O'Donnell had briefly considered becoming a talk-show host in 1993. After substituting for Kathie Lee

Gifford on *Live with Regis and Kathie Lee* in 1995, she was hooked, and she decided to take a shot at hosting her own program. By the end of the year, she had a contract with Warner Bros. to produce and star in *The Rosie O'Donnell Show*, scheduled to debut the following June during TV's off-season so that it would have a better chance with audiences.

The decision to base the show in New York was a boon for Rosie. Most of her immediate family still lived in the area; not only would she see more of them, but Parker would also have the benefit of seeing his cousins, aunts, and uncles more frequently. One of O'Donnell's first acts as the executive producer of her show was to create a soundproof office and nursery where Parker could rest and play while she taped her shows.

As it turned out, the studio where *The Rosie O'Donnell Show* is shot is the former setting of one of her

"Merv Griffin for the '90s": talk-show host Rosie O'Donnell accepts a plate of cookies and an autographed baseball from Sister Mary Assumpta (right). On the left is Sister Marguerite Torre, older sibling of New York Yankees manager Joe Torre.

O'Donnell harmonizes with pal Madonna, right, on The Rosie O'Donnell Show. *Rosie's friendship with Madonna introduced her to the difficulties of being a celebrity long before she herself became a star. She is especially protective of her children, Parker Jaren and Chelsea Belle. "Fame is a very difficult thing for an adult to deal with," she says, "and it's nearly impossible for a child to understand."*

favorite programs from childhood, the *Phil Donahue Show*. She would later learn from one of her guests that during the 1960s, it was also the setting for *The Tonight Show*, before Johnny Carson took the program to California.

The *Rosie O'Donnell Show* was an immediate success. Its June 10 debut episode earned a Nielsen rating of 3.2, one of the highest opening Nielsen scores ever—second only to the *The Oprah Winfrey Show*. (Nielsen is a standard ratings system for television that measures a show's popularity in two ways: first, among all households that own televisions, and second, in "audience shares," or the percentage of households in which televisions are not only turned on but also tuned to the show. Each point in the ratings represents one percent of television households in the United States, or 980,000 households.) After a month, Rosie's show reached 3.9. And in New York, 23 percent of households watching television had the show on during its time slot.

By mid-July, *The Rosie O'Donnell Show* became the fifth-highest-rated daytime TV talk show in America. *Newsweek* magazine featured O'Donnell on its cover and gave her a new nickname: the Queen of Nice. Comparing Rosie's success to Oprah Winfrey's number one-rated talk show, *Adweek* magazine said, "Rosie and Oprah are two strong examples of how a show can successfully balance the scales between achieving high ratings and maintaining a quality environment." Across the country, local TV stations that originally scheduled *The Rosie O'Donnell Show* for odd or late-night hours began upgrading the program to prime spots like mid-morning or mid-afternoon so that they could raise ad fees for commercial sponsors. By fall 1996, Warner Bros. had guaranteed Rosie's show through the 1999-2000 season.

Despite a number of staff changes in its first two years of production, *The Rosie O'Donnell Show* has grown increasingly popular. At the end of 1997, it was consistently the second-highest-rated daytime talk show in America. Among key groups, such as women aged 18 to 34, Rosie ranks equally with Oprah Winfrey. And in May 1998, *The Rosie O'Donnell Show* won two Emmy awards, including Outstanding Talk Show. Rosie herself shared a third award for Outstanding Talk Show Host with Oprah Winfrey.

On November 12, 1997, Rosie announced to a delighted TV audience that she had adopted a baby girl, Chelsea Belle, born September 20. True to form, Rosie followed the advice of her favorite children in naming her new daughter—one of her nieces suggested the name Chelsea, and the lead in Parker's favorite movie, Disney's *Beauty and the Beast*, is named Belle.

Although Chelsea's arrival meant that Rosie had to turn down a promising movie role or two, she couldn't be happier about her growing family. She says that the support of family and friends allows her to continue her talk-show career while raising two children.

Achieving the level of fame that Rosie O'Donnell has reached nearly always comes with a loss of privacy. Going about their daily routines, and even in their own homes, celebrities often find themselves in the spotlight, sought after by photographers and reporters attempting to satisfy the curiosity of the public. Some stars accept this as part of the territory that comes with fame; others believe that achieving fame doesn't require you to give up your private life. Perhaps the greatest backlash against such invasions of privacy came in September 1997, when the paparazzi (freelance photographers) pursuing Diana, Princess of Wales, were blamed in part for causing the Paris auto accident that took her life. In any event, at one time or another, probably all celebrities have wished for the peace and solitude of a non-public life, despite the benefits of being famous.

Rosie O'Donnell experienced a number of intrusions into her private life, especially after Parker was born. A photo of mother and son was in great demand. One day while at home visiting with a friend, Rosie spotted a man standing in her yard pointing a camera at her. "I'm sorry," he told her, "[b]ut they offered me this much money. I'll leave, but people will be back." Rosie agreed to let him take a few pictures, and in return he agreed not to show her son's face in the photos.

Being friends with a high-profile celebrity such as Madonna had made O'Donnell familiar with the perils of fame. Early on in their friendship, Rosie was astonished at the degree to which facts become distorted or invented as tabloids and other media constantly seek fresh news on America's hottest stars. She recalled her surprise when she heard a TV show report that Madon-

na had flown to New York the previous evening to dine with Donald Trump—on the morning after Rosie and Madonna had gone out for a quiet dinner together. "This was my first experience with the press announcing something that simply was not [true]," Rosie said.

Some time before Princess Diana's death in 1997, actor George Clooney (star of TV's *ER* and the movies *Batman & Robin* and *The Peacemaker*) launched a boycott of TV tabloid news by refusing to give interviews to *Entertainment Tonight* (*ET*) and a similar program, *Hard Copy*, both of which are owned by Paramount Pictures. Clooney hoped that if a number of stars refused to give interviews, Paramount would feel pressured to back off. His supporters included Madonna, Whoopi Goldberg, Steven Spielberg, and Rosie O'Don-

O'Donnell records a character voice for the California Prune Board's animated TV ads in 1997. Rosie donated her $350,000 fee to breast cancer research organizations.

nell herself, who canceled an interview she had scheduled with *ET*. Some celebrity photographers fought back by "boycotting" Clooney, refusing to take his picture even during scheduled publicity appearances.

On her talk show, in guest appearances, and during interviews, Rosie speaks openly about her children and how fame has affected all of their lives. But the stories she shares with the public are usually amusing tales that most mothers tell about their children and do not involve what Rosie believes to be an invasion of her children's privacy. In a TV interview with Naomi Judd in October 1996, for example, she proudly described 17-month-old Parker's development. "He's saying 'Mommy' every day—regular, loud and frequent," she joked. But she refuses to "show off" her children on the air. "Fame is tough enough on me. On a child, it can be impossible."

O'Donnell has also learned that with fame comes enormous influence. The vast popularity of *The Rosie O'Donnell Show* attracts the attention of corporations that are eager to stay on Rosie's good side. One day, for example, Rosie lamented on the air that the brand of diapers she used, Pampers Premium, had been discontinued by the company. She urged them to reconsider. As it turned out, Pampers was simply redesigning the product, and the company eventually sent her several cases of the new version. She was also partly responsible for the huge 1996 Christmas rush for Tyco's Tickle Me Elmo doll, which she featured on her show (in 1997, Tyco released a talking "Rosie O'Doll" in her honor).

Another corporate coup came in 1997 when Procter & Gamble, the makers of Scope mouthwash, released a list of "kissable" and "unkissable" celebrities, naming O'Donnell among the latter. In response, Rosie and her writers launched a full-scale attack on Scope, declaring frequently that Listerine, Scope's market rival, was the better product. Unfortunately for Procter

Tony Awards host Rosie O'Donnell performs with cast members of Rent, Grease!, *and other Broadway shows during the 1997 awards ceremony at Radio City Music Hall.*

& Gamble, the makers of Listerine were watching, and they offered to contribute $1,000 to O'Donnell's For All Kids Foundation for disadvantaged children each time she kissed a guest on the air. For weeks, nearly everyone on the show gave Rosie at least one peck on the cheek. Each time, a counter would appear on viewers' screens that tallied the current pledge total. According to the October 1997 issue of *Us* magazine, the campaign raised $500,000.

Knowing that O'Donnell is a great collector of TV-show and movie merchandise, her fans and her guests often go to great lengths to give her rare or unusual memorabilia. One fan who knew about Rosie's adoration for the soap opera *Ryan's Hope* threw a jacket emblazoned with the show's logo into the talk-show host's car as Rosie drove away from a charity flea market. Rosie thanked the anonymous woman on the air the following day. On Rosie's 101st show, Disney and McDonald's surprised her with a full set of the 101 Dalmatian figurines McDonald's was distributing to promote Disney's film. Marlo Thomas, the star of one of Rosie's favorite 1970s sitcoms, *That Girl*, gave Rosie a replica of the pink kite she flew in the show's opening credits—but instead of its *That Girl* logo, the kite was stamped with the cartoon image used to open *The Rosie O'Donnell Show*.

At the same time, O'Donnell is known for showing appreciation for her fans and guests. Each day, members of her audience find a carton of low-fat milk and a package of Drake's cakes on their seats—Rosie's effort to make the studio feel more homelike. She has welcomed a number of guests, including supermodel Cindy Crawford, in the same way by handing them Drake products (the Drake company, of course, is delighted), and she often surprises her guests by displaying items from her vast collection of show-business memorabilia that relate to them. Marlo Thomas, for example, was shown an aged edition of *TV Guide* that featured her on its cover. And when singer and actress Cher was scheduled, Rosie produced a Cher doll—complete with the botched haircut she had given it when she was 12 years old.

Rosie also loves to make her studio audience, and by extension her viewers at home, feel involved in the show. Each day, a member of the audience introduces the talk-show host. Kooshball attacks and competitions are common—the soft, spiky rubber toy has become an O'Donnell trademark. (The company even came out with a special Rosie edition Kooshball in 1996.)

In fact, the trait most admired by critics and fans alike is the star's accessibility. O'Donnell regularly appears after each show to sign autographs for kids and talk with her fans. She often announces her upcoming appear-

ances at fund-raisers, concerts, and other events, which draw larger than usual crowds as a result. In the New York area, she is often seen in public while shopping or running errands and is usually glad to spend a moment with her fans. O'Donnell also loves to answer fan mail. Although she can't respond to each letter, she has put her childhood pal Jackie Ellard to work sorting through the huge volume of fan mail she receives each day, to be sure that each letter gets some measure of attention.

Rosie is also a regular on the America Online (AOL) chat forum, having become "hooked" on the Internet during the filming of *Another Stakeout*, where most of the cast and crew were AOL members. Here, too, she receives thousands of E-mails each day from devoted fans. *The Rosie O'Donnell Show* also has its own website

Rosie's lifelong admiration for Barbra Streisand was evident in her emotional interview with the singer and actress on the November 19, 1997, edition of The Rosie O'Donnell Show.

(http://www.rosieo.com/), complete with "Cutie-Patootie Parenting Tips" and a "Contact Rosie" page. Of course, the official talk-show site is only one of many Rosie O'Donnell websites that have sprung up since her program debuted in 1996.

Rosie's great love and concern for children is evident in the way she responds to her fans. She has one rule about answering mail and signing autographs: kids come first. She gives autographs only to children, preferring simply to shake hands and speak with adults instead. And though she will respond to E-mails and letters from grown-ups, she does so only after she has addressed the kids' mail. Naomi Serviss of *Newsday* summed up Rosie's appeal to youngsters and parents: "What other live show can you take kids to where they'll see a good-natured, normal-looking celebrity? None. . . . *The Rosie O'Donnell Show* loves kids, with staffers scanning ticket holders looking for wee ones to make announcements and showcase artistic talents and singing skills."

Hosting her own talk show is not Rosie's only project. She still makes guest appearances at charity fund-raisers, especially for her most cherished causes: AIDS research, breast cancer awareness, and children's health and welfare. Shortly before her show debuted, Rosie appeared with Linda Ellerbee in a Nickelodeon program called "The Body Trap." The special, part of the award-winning program *Nick News*, gave kids the chance to discuss their feelings about their looks, helped to explain the ways that physical appearance can affect one's feeling of self-worth, and examined the ways in which the media shapes these ideas. In April 1997 Rosie published the book *Kids Are Punny*, a collection of jokes by kids that reached number two on the *Wall Street Journal*'s nonfiction bestseller list. In February 1998, she was named as host and producer of the 52nd Annual Tony Awards. Two months later, she once again hosted Nickelodeon's Annual Kids' Choice

Awards after having received the favorite movie actress award twice (in 1995 for *The Flintstones* and in 1997 for *Harriet the Spy*). She has also provided a character voice for TV commercials promoting California prunes and is considering a role as Totie Fields in a movie about the actress's life.

Rosie O'Donnell may be famous, but her feet are planted firmly in reality. Even when welcoming the biggest names in Hollywood to her show, she can seem like a starstruck member of the audience. And while she is aware that stardom brings power and influence, she also knows that it can be fleeting. "For a while, everybody likes the underdog," she said after appearing in her first two movies:

> But you know, after a while you're not the underdog anymore. Then you're the one who always gets up to bat and hits. Then they're like, "Enough, already. Oh, you think you're so great now?" . . . Especially if you change, if you start to become different than what it was [people] fell in love with to begin with. It's hard to maintain that. . . . Your act has to change as your life changes. . . . otherwise the audience is lost, and they end up resenting you.

But fame is not the driving force in Rosie's life. Her friends and family—especially her children, Parker and Chelsea—keep her grounded. She is determined to raise her kids just as any normal mother would, despite the trappings of success. And her broad appeal is a testament to her down-to-earth nature.

Rosie knows that one day her popularity will fade, but that's okay with her. Though she has plans to try her hand at film directing, she also hopes one day to retire and become what she calls a "full-time mom." Being famous, she said in 1997, is like catching "a big wave . . . till it hits the surf, and then when you're done, you say, 'Thanks, that was great.'" For now, Rosie O'Donnell is content to ride the wave.

CHRONOLOGY

1962   Roseann (Rosie) O'Donnell born on March 21 in Commack, NY

1973   Rosie's mother, Roseann O'Donnell, dies of cancer on March 17

1978   Wins $50 performing her first stand-up act at a local restaurant; begins professional stand-up career at a Long Island comedy club

1980   Graduates from high school; begins college at Dickinson

1981   Transfers to Boston University; leaves after one semester

1982   Joins Eastside Comedy Club's Laughter Company; begins traveling the East Coast comedy circuit

1984   Appears on TV's *Star Search*

1986-87 Stars in the TV sitcom *Gimme a Break*

1988   Becomes veejay for VH-1; appears on Showtime's *Comedy Club Network*

1989   Named host and executive producer of VH-1's *Stand-Up Spotlight*

1990   Stars in *Car 54, Where Are You?* (the movie is released in 1994)

1992   Appears in the movie *A League of Their Own;* stars opposite Melissa Gilbert in the TV program *Stand By Your Man*

1993   Appears in *Sleepless in Seattle* and *Another Stakeout*

1994   Stars in *The Flintstones* and *Exit to Eden;* premieres on Broadway in *Grease!;* appears in *Now and Then*

1995   Appears in *Beautiful Girls;* wins the Nickelodeon Kids' Choice Award for Favorite Movie Actress; adopts Parker Jaren, born May 25; receives her first Emmy nomination for Outstanding Individual Performance in a Variety or Music Program

1996   Appears in *Harriet the Spy; The Rosie O'Donnell Show* debuts on June 10; makes cameo appearance as herself in *A Very Brady Sequel*

1997   Wins second Nickelodeon Kids' Choice Award; appears in Showtime movie *Twilight of the Golds;* publishes *Kids Are Punny;* adopts a second child, Chelsea Belle, born September 20; wins Emmy for Outstanding Talk Show Host

1998   Produces and hosts the 52nd Annual Tony Awards; appears in *Wide Awake;* shares Emmy award for Outstanding Talk Show Host with Oprah Winfrey; *The Rosie O'Donnell Show* awarded Outstanding Talk Show Emmy

1999   Lends vocal talents to animated film *Tarzan*; adopts Blake Christopher, born December 5

2000   Hosts 42nd Annual Grammy Awards and 54th Annual Tony Awards

FILMOGRAPHY

FILM

A League of Their Own (1992)

Another Stakeout (1993)

Sleepless in Seattle (1993)

Car 54, Where Are You? (1994)

Exit to Eden (1994)

The Flintstones (1994)

I'll Do Anything (1994)

Now and Then (1995)

Beautiful Girls (1996)

Harriet the Spy (1996)

A Very Brady Sequel (1996)

Twilight of the Golds (Showtime, 1997)

Wide Awake (1998)

Tarzan (voice, 1999)

TELEVISION

Star Search (contestant, 1984)

Gimme a Break (series, 1986–1987)

Stand-Up Spotlight (host, producer, 1989–1993)

A Pair of Jokers: Bill Engvall & Rosie O'Donnell (1990)

Women Aloud (guest appearance, 1992)

Back to School '92 (host, 1992)

Stand by Your Man (series, 1992)

Beverly Hills, 90210 (guest appearance, 1992)

The Flintstones: Best of Bedrock (host, 1994)

The Cindy Crawford Special (MTV, guest appearance, 1994)

Living Single (guest appearance, 1994)

Rosie O'Donnell (HBO comedy special, 1995)

Night Stand (guest appearance, 1995)

Bless This House (guest appearance, 1995)

The Larry Sanders Show (guest appearance, 1995)

The Good, the Bad, and the Beautiful (cohost, 1996)

Ninth Annual Kids' Choice Awards (host, 1996)

Nick News Special Edition: The Body Trap (cohost, 1996)

The Rosie O'Donnell Show (host, executive producer, 1996–present)

All My Children (guest appearance, 1996)

The Nanny (two guest appearances, 1996)

Saturday Night Live (host, 1996)

Suddenly Susan (guest appearance, 1997)

Wheel of Fortune (guest appearance, 1997)

10th Annual Kids' Choice Awards (host, 1997)

51st Annual Antoinette Perry (Tony) Awards (host, 1997)

Say It, Fight It, Cure It (guest appearance, 1997)

11th Annual Kids' Choice Awards (host, 1998)

Murphy Brown (guest appearance, 1998)

52nd Annual Antoinette Perry (Tony) Awards (host, producer, 1998)

42nd Annual Grammy Awards (host, 2000)

54th Annual Antoinette Perry (Tony) Awards (host, producer, 2000)

THEATER

Grease! (1994)

BIBLIOGRAPHY

Bellafante, Ginia. "The Rosie O'Donnell Show." *Time*, 24 June 1996.

Berryhill, Ken. *Funny Business*. Englewood Cliffs, NJ: Prentice Hall, 1985.

Cahill, Gloria. "The Serious Side of Rosie O'Donnell." *Radiance*, December 1997.

Flaim, Denise. "Really Rosie's." *Newsday*, Sunday Home Section, 5 May 1996.

Gallo, Hank. *Comedy Explosion*. New York: Thunder Mouth Press, 1991.

Garey, Julian. "Rosie the Riveting." *Entertainment Weekly*, 7 August 1992.

Glico, Jeff. "Playing in a League of Her Own." *Newsweek*, 16 August 1992.

Mair, George, and Anna Green. *Rosie O'Donnell: Her True Story*. Secaucus, NJ: Birch Lane Press, 1997.

Marin, Rick. "Queen of Nice—Coming Up Rosies." *Newsweek*, 15 July 1996.

Mr. Showbiz (Internet), "Rosie O'Donnell." *Star Bios*, 5 September 1996.

Mr. Showbiz (Internet), "Rosie O'Donnell Adopts Daughter." *News Review: Hollywood Headlines*, 13 November 1997.

Mr. Showbiz (Internet), "Rosie's Return Tony Engagement." *News Review: Hollywood Headlines*, 10 December 1997.

Mr. Showbiz (Internet), "Rosie Scores Big with Streisand." *News Review: Hollywood Headlines*, 25 November 1997.

Murphy, Mary. "Rosie, Really." *TV Guide*, 15 June 1996.

Parish, James Robert. *Rosie: Rosie O'Donnell's Biography*. New York: Carroll & Graf Publishers, 1997.

Smith, Liz. "Really Rosie." *Good Housekeeping*, June 1997.

Spahn, Paula. "Lending Talk TV a Sympathetic Ear." *Washington Post*, 30 November 1997.

Udovitch, Mimi. "Rosie O'Donnell." *Us*, October 1997.

INDEX

Fran Donato is originally from Springfield, Pennsylvania. She attended Penn State University and the University of Mississippi, majoring in communications.

Therese De Angelis holds an M.A. in English Literature from Villanova University. She was the contributing editor for Chelsea House's *The Black Muslims* and the WOMEN WRITERS OF ENGLISH series. She is also the author of *Native Americans and the Spanish* in the INDIANS OF NORTH AMERICA series and *Louis Farrakhan* in the BLACK AMERICANS OF ACHIEVEMENT series.

Matina S. Horner was president of Radcliffe College and associate professor of psychology and social relations at Harvard University. She is best known for her studies of women's motivation, achievement, and personality development. Dr. Horner has served on several national boards and advisory councils, including those of the National Science Foundation, Time Inc., and the Women's Research and Education Institute. She earned her B.A. from Bryn Mawr College and her Ph.D. from the University of Michigan, and holds honorary degrees from many colleges and universities, including Mount Holyoke, Smith, Tufts, and the University of Pennsylvania.

PICTURE CREDITS